Songs of Power and Prayer in the Columbia Plateau

Native Ancestral Lands and Jesuit Missions in the Columbia Plateau, 1847

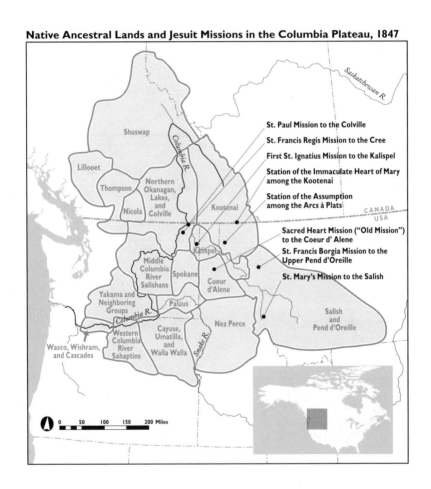

Songs of Power and Prayer in the Columbia Plateau

The Jesuit,
the Medicine Man,
and the Indian Hymn Singer

Chad Stephen Hamill

Oregon State University Press: Corvallis

FIRST PEOPLES
New Directions in Indigenous Studies

Publication of this book was made possible, in part, with a grant from the Andrew W. Mellon Foundation.

Visit www.osupress.oregonstate.edu for supplemental materials, including streaming audio recordings

Cover art: "Salish Lord," was painted by Mrs. O. Wiprud in 1955 as a gift for the church at St. Ignatius Mission on the Flathead reservation. *Musical notation:* unknown, n.d. (cf. ILC: Kalispel Coll.) Jesuit Oregon Province Archives, Gonzaga University.

The paper in this book meets the guidelines for permanence and durability of the Committee on Production Guidelines for Book Longevity of the Council on Library Resources and the minimum requirements of the American National Standard for Permanence of Paper for Printed Library Materials Z39.48-1984.

Library of Congress Cataloging-in-Publication Data
Hamill, Chad Stephen.
  Songs of power and prayer in the Columbia Plateau : the Jesuit, the medicine man, and the Indian hymn singer / by Chad Stephen Hamill.
    p. cm.
  Includes bibliographical references and index.
  ISBN 978-0-87071-675-1 (pbk. : alk. paper) -- ISBN 978-0-87071-676-8 (e-book)
  1. Spokane Indians--Music--History and criticism. 2. Spokane Indians--Missions. 3. Spokane Indians--Religion. 4. Spokane Indians--Cultural assimilation. 5. Jesuits--Missions--Columbia Plateau. 6. Indian Catholics--Columbia Plateau--History. I. Title.
  ML3557.H36 2012
  782.42162'97943--dc23
                                    2011052246

First published in 2012 by Oregon State University Press
Printed in the United States of America

Oregon State University Press
121 The Valley Library
Corvallis OR 97331-4501
541-737-3166 • fax 541-737-3170
www.osupress.oregonstate.edu

Contents

Preface

My first encounter with indigenous music of the Columbia Plateau region took place during a Native American music course at the University of Colorado, where I was laboring toward a PhD in ethnomusicology. I viewed the course as an opportunity to focus on music I wished to know but had for too long neglected. My initial search for information, fueled by an abiding interest in my own Native Plateau ancestry, continually led me back to Dr. Loran Olsen, a professor emeritus from Washington State University. Thirty-five years earlier, Dr. William Elmendorf, an anthropologist active in indigenous Northwest culture studies, had handed Dr. Olsen five reel-to-reel tapes of Niimiipuu (Nez Perce) songs he had recorded.[1] From that point forward Dr. Olsen's role as a professor of piano and theory took on a different hue as he gradually began to display characteristics common to a then fairly rare musical species known as the *ethnomusicologist*.

Armed with a recorder and a notepad, he traversed the Columbia Plateau, conducting fieldwork and working alongside the Niimiipuu and other tribes to preserve songs that might have otherwise faded away. In addition to producing numerous articles that have illuminated central features of indigenous Plateau song, Dr. Olsen established the Nez Perce Music Archive, a collection of hundreds of songs recorded over the past one hundred years and a monograph on a Plateau song genre known as *Qillóowawya* ("hitting the rawhide"), which includes recordings of songs that have largely fallen out of use. After directing the focus of my dissertation toward indigenous music of the Columbia Plateau region, there was but one place to turn. I gave Dr. Olsen a call. It went something like this:

HAMILL: [*somewhat rehearsed*] Hello, Dr. Olsen, my name is Chad
    Hamill. I am a PhD student in ethnomusicology at the University
    of Colorado doing research on traditional music of the Columbia
    Plateau region. I have Native Plateau ancestry myself and

would like to produce something that will be of value to future generations of Plateau people.

OLSEN: Well, I've been waiting for you to call. I have a bunch of stuff here that I just don't have time to get to, and I need someone to pick up on it.

HAMILL: [*a bit stunned*] Oh . . . Okay, when can we get together?

OLSEN: I'm here in Port Angeles, Washington. You can come anytime.

As soon as I was able to wrap up courses that semester, I loaded the family (including the dog) in the car and drove from Boulder, Colorado, to Port Angeles. Early in our initial conversations, Dr. Olsen provided a long list of people I needed to contact during my research period. He labeled certain individuals as high priority—those "you need to contact as soon as possible!" Among them was Father Tom Connolly, a Jesuit who had been working within indigenous Plateau communities for half a century. After a few days I left with a list of names, numbers, and other materials, beginning the fieldwork phase of my research in earnest.

During initial trips from Colorado to the Plateau region, I took the opportunity to do some genealogical research. My great-great-grandfather was Spokan and went by the Indian name "Squ'elta" (Red Sun).[2] At some point during the period of acculturation among the Spokan, he adopted the Christian title "James Elijah," at times reducing the last name to "Eli." He met my great-great-grandmother, Hattie Colsen, in Dayton, Washington, in 1889. Oral accounts within my family tell of two people drawn together by a mutual interest in horses. Dayton was well known for horse racing during the time, a history that predated Euro-American contact (after the introduction of the horse in the eighteenth century, Native people of the Plateau conducted horse races where Dayton now sits, on a course that would eventually become Main Street). During a fieldwork trip in March 2006, I headed up to the tribal office on the Spokane reservation and met with the tribal genealogist. During prior research, I had come across references to Gibson Eli, often referred to as "the last medicine man of the Spokan tribe." Given the "Eli" surname, I suspected I might be related to him.

The tribal genealogist confirmed that we were: Gibson was the son of James Elijah and the half brother of my great-grandmother, Lulu Colsen.

During our conversation, she mentioned she had a tape of Eli singing some of his songs. Not sure exactly where it was kept, she said she would have a copy ready for me on my next visit the following month. When I returned, she had a small pile of items assembled, including materials on Spokan history and culture so, as she said, "you can learn more about your tribe." Lost to my family was a link, buried deep beneath the weight of generations and the accumulation of time. During the melee of cultural chaos and confusion in the early twentieth century, an ancestral artery was torn. It began to heal that day.

After an emotional goodbye, I made my way from the tribal office in Wellpinit back to my home in Colorado. I remember handling the cassette with care, as one might handle a precious and delicate artifact. I couldn't help but think that it held something for my ears only; that it would tell me something about my ancestral past while directing me toward a future I could only begin to imagine. Unfortunately, it was a *lousy* recording. While I could make out the melody of the songs, the words Eli spoke were barely intelligible, flooded by tape hiss and background noise. It was an interview of sorts—discussion interspersed with song. As I struggled with pained determination to make out what Eli was saying, I thought I heard him utter the name "Father Connolly." I played the same section again and again, until I was certain I was hearing it right. Could it be the same person mentioned by Dr. Olsen? How could it *not* be?

As I approached the Mission of the Sacred Heart, stationed like a noble sentry atop a hill overlooking the camas prairie on the Coeur d'Alene reservation, I wondered what a Jesuit would be able to tell me about "the last medicine man of the Spokan tribe." While discussing his medicine dance on the cassette tape,[3] Eli could be heard stating something to the effect of "Ask Father Connolly . . . He'll tell you anything." By "anything," did he mean *everything*? What could a Jesuit possibly know about the inner workings of a Spokan healer and his medicine dance? I recalled the first time I had heard Eli's advice on the tape: his words about Father Connolly suggested that their relationship had been unconventional, perhaps occupying some space in between the pronounced polarity commonly associated with indigenous healers and Christian missionaries. Of course, it was also possible that Eli had been trying to throw the interviewers off, playfully sending them to the *last* person who could entertain questions about his use of medicine power. Ultimately, I decided that whether or not Connolly knew intimate details was unimportant, as long as he could shed some light on the man I didn't know in life but was hoping to get to know now.

Connolly greeted me at the door with an infectious energy I might have associated with someone half his age (he was approaching eighty at the time). As he politely ushered me to the kitchen table, his jovial demeanor quickly gave way to sobriety as he picked up a pen and paper and asked me to trace my relation to Eli. He produced a stack of genealogy charts, pulling one that started with James Elijah and Eli's mom, a dense family tree that stretched all the way to Eli's grandchildren. Over the course of an hour or so, the questions kept coming, and our meeting began to feel like a cordial interrogation. I told Connolly everything I knew about my family history, about my fieldwork and my overall motivation. I explained that I was interested in doing meaningful research, not simply in service of a particular academic discipline but for future generations of Plateau people. This led to a conversation about Columbia Plateau history. He was very knowledgeable and had great things to share, but I was becoming anxious. How well did he actually know Eli?

As the conversation waned and the gaps of silent reflection grew wider, he got up and invited me back to his office. Walking over to a file cabinet, he started to take out various files, placing them on top of one another. When all the files were stacked and the pile was high, he began to share their contents. They contained pictures, newspaper clippings, and countless handwritten notes assembled over two decades—all of it concerning Eli and his friend Mitch Michael, a Spokan/Coeur d'Alene Indian prayer leader. I could see that Connolly was fielding memories as he went through the different items, each carrying him to a time and place that had passed but remained alive in his heart. More than casual acquaintances, Connolly and Eli were dear friends. I started to think that I might have been right about the tape; through the hiss and noise stood weathered signposts of an ancestral past pointing me toward a path that would begin here, oddly enough, in Connolly's office at the Sacred Heart mission. On that day my research in the Columbia Plateau broadened to include a great-uncle I was just beginning to know, through the notes and recollections of his friend and spiritual ally.

My desire to learn about Eli was about more than genealogy. Years before I entertained the notion of pursuing a PhD in ethnomusicology, I had participated in indigenous North American ceremonies, continually engaging with phenomena often referred to, in Native terms, as "power." In the late 1990s I began dancing in a Ghost Dance on the San Pasqual reservation in Southern California, a process through which my engagement with power increased. I soon found myself enveloped by it. In addition to manifesting in the dance arbor, it inhabited my dreams, blurring the lines between the material and ethereal realms. I knew on some level my experiences were tied to my Native ancestry, but I longed to know exactly how. I was hoping my "search" for Gibson Eli might reveal what a two-dimensional chart could not—facets of the multidimensional presence of power in my own life.

Just when it seemed Connolly's recollections might shed some light on these questions, my foray into ancestry and spiritual power took an unexpected turn. Within the pictures, newspaper clippings, and extensive notes was a story in need of telling. Connolly and his "two grandfathers," Mitch Michael and Gibson Eli, had formed an uncommon bond, crossing religious and spiritual lines in a collective search for the sacred. In the process, they upended notions of indigeneity and tradition, rewriting the rules of engagement for priests and Indians in the Columbia Plateau.

Critical to their efforts was an element I knew well as an ethnomusicologist. While locating the sacred may have been their primary aim, song was their primary vehicle. I would soon discover that the Indian hymn leader sang Catholic hymns in Salish, the priest sang medicine songs during indigenous healings, and the medicine man sang indigenous songs during Catholic services. Whether in the context of indigenous ceremonies or Catholic rituals, song was essential, dissolving difference and sounding the sacred.

Acknowledgments

Only through the generosity and support of many has this singular work been possible. I have received critical guidance from exceptional teachers during this process, both within the academy and in the Columbia Plateau.

I owe a considerable debt of gratitude to Loran Olsen, without whom my work in the Columbia Plateau would not have been possible. Thanks, Loran, for being a facilitator, mentor, and friend. You have demonstrated that research can make a difference.

I would like to thank other Columbia Plateau scholars who have become role models, setting the highest standards for research while maintaining close relationships with Plateau people: Deward Walker, Ron Pond, and Bruce Rigsby.

Within the field of ethnomusicology, I would like to thank ethnomusicologists Charlotte Frisbie and Victoria Lindsay Levine for their critical guidance early in the publication process.

A special thanks goes to Johnny Arlee, who was instrumental in illuminating the lines of correspondence (as well as lost opportunities) between the first Jesuits and Native communities in the Plateau.

To all those in Native communities who opened their doors and their hearts in the Plateau: thank you for your trust. With the words contained herein I have strived to create something of enduring value to future generations. I look forward to our continued work together toward this end.

I would also like to thank Father Tom Connolly for sharing his story and for the opportunity to help share it with others.

To Mary Braun and all the folks at OSU Press and the First Peoples Initiative, thanks for gently and adroitly guiding an author toward the realization of his first book.

To my parents, Janice and Stephen Hamill, thank you for instilling within me a sense that I could do anything, even while I chose to do nothing but music.

And to Betsy, who gave me the room to do what I needed to do and never asked why, thank you for your tremendous grace throughout this process. You are the answer to a prayer. I look forward to getting on with the business of shaping our land, raising our boys, and changing the world.

Introduction

Comprehensive studies into the relationship between song and spirituality are few. Scholars have acknowledged song as important, perhaps even integral to spiritual processes, but inquiry often ends there. While participating in the Ghost Dance, I encountered in a very direct way the use of song as a catalyst for spiritual power (Hamill 2008), experiencing a phenomenon that for millennia has been central to the spiritual lives of Native people. While it may be true that an ethnomusicologist such as myself is inclined to privilege "musical" phenomena over others, the essential role of song in indigenous North American ceremonies is indisputable, for without a thing called song there *is* no ceremony. As far back as 1965 Alan Merriam, one of the founders of the field of ethnomusicology, recognized the necessity of song within the ceremonial sphere as well as a need for more substantive inquiry into its relationship to spiritual praxis, a need that remains largely unfulfilled. Speaking to the phenomena of "song acquisition" in the vision quest, he states, "The acquisition of song in these contacts with the supernatural, particularly in connection with the vision quest, has often been commented upon, but its importance to the total experience has not received the stress it deserves. In many respects, song is the central concern in the quest; it is through the conferring of the song or songs that the experience is made meaningful and that the powers conferred by the guardian spirit are made operative" (1965:95).

Merriam's thoughts on song as the primary catalyst for the manifestation of spiritual power highlight a phenomenon that is a critical component of indigenous ceremonies throughout North America and throughout the world.[1] While exploring the individual and collective spaces within the spectrum of Catholic and indigenous ritual, I intend to give song the "stress it deserves," not just as a conduit or catalyst for spiritual power but as the singular thread that ties the narrative of *Songs of Power and Prayer in the Columbia Plateau* together. Whether the first Catholic hymn sung in Salish by the Coeur d'Alene in the nineteenth century, an ancient indigenous death chant adapted to the Catholic wake, or a medicine song to purge an individual of a terminal disease, song was critical to realizing the ritual. As such, it is within the song that we find the story.

Song and Identity

The first official Catholic emissary to the Columbia Plateau was a young Jesuit by the name of Pierre-Jean DeSmet. His initial trip west from St. Louis in 1840 was a response to numerous entreaties made by indigenous Plateau people, who sent four delegations to St. Louis throughout the 1830s in a perilous but determined effort to bring "Blackrobes" to the Plateau region. After erecting the first mission among the Salish in 1841,[2] Father DeSmet and his Jesuit recruits built a string of missions in the interior Northwest, erecting missions for the Coeur d'Alene in 1842, the Kalispel in 1844, and the Colville in 1845. As part of his vision to establish an "empire of Christian Indians" (Peterson and Peers 1993:23), DeSmet and his fellow Jesuits set about translating Catholic hymns into Interior Salish, a method by which they sought to indoctrinate indigenous Columbia Plateau people.[3] Rather than Catholicizing Indians, however, the hymns were themselves indigenized—absorbed, reconstructed, and re-sung as expressions of Native identity.

In his landmark work, *Putting a Song on Top of It: Expression and Identity on the Apache San Carlos Reservation,* David Samuels explores seemingly contradictory expressions of Apache identity enacted through rock, reggae, and country music, challenging popular notions of Native American culture as staunch and steadfastly anachronistic. Speaking to expressive forms of culture, Samuels finds that "the relationships between cultures and identities are not fixed. Rather, identities are emergent, produced out of the practices and expressive forms of everyday life. Traditions are not simply handed along from one generation to the next. Part of their enduring power comes from the possibility of their strategic reinvention in order to speak strongly in new social and political contexts" (2004:5). While leading Catholic Indian hymns,

Mitch Michael was doing more than expressing Christian sentiments, he was invoking over one hundred years of collective indigenous identity within which the strands of Catholicism were woven into the fabric of an indigenous Coeur d'Alene worldview. The Coeur d'Alene became Catholics, this is true, but they were and would always be Indian.

Tracing the historical interactions between Russian Orthodox missionaries and the Tlingit people at the turn of the twentieth century, Sergei Kan found that a "growing body of ethnohistorical research shows that North American Indians have often reinterpreted Christian ideas, rituals, and institutions, and that their approach to Christianity has been selective, creative, and synthesizing. Christianity, as a result, frequently became *indigenized*" (1985:196 [original italics]). This perspective paints a picture contrary to the one with which we are most familiar, of indigenous people as beleaguered and helpless in the face of inexorable Christian forces. Instead, it acknowledges individual and collective indigenous agency within a process of cultural and religious negotiation, whereby indigenous identity, or indigeneity, remains firmly intact.

It might be said that the first Jesuits in the Columbia Plateau region were unwitting partners in this process of Catholic indigenization. Although their efforts to cultivate communities of good Indian Christians were more accommodating than those of their Protestant and Methodist counterparts, cultural repression, whether direct or indirect, was employed as a tool of conversion. When intractable "Indian" characteristics or objects stood in the way, attempts were made to dispose of them. At the early missions, indigenous ceremonies were discouraged or simply banned, and medicines used in non-Christian spiritual contexts, including medicine bundles, were buried or destroyed. Quoting Father Nicholas Point, his Jesuit compatriot in the Rocky Mountain mission enterprise, DeSmet writes that "from Christmas to Candlemas, the missionary's fire was kept up with all that remained of the ancient 'medicine.' It was a beautiful sight to behold the principal supporters of it, with their own hands destroy the wretched instruments which hell had employed, to deceive their ignorance or give credit to their impostures. And in the long winter evenings, how many birds feathers, wolves' tails, feet of hinds, hoofs of deers, bits of cloth, wooded images, and other superstitious objects were sacrificed!" (1985:32).

What the Jesuits perhaps failed to anticipate was the ingenuity and resilience of the cultures they encountered, comprising indigenous identities both fluid and "emergent." Despite Point's assertion, much "remained" of the old medicine ways during the process of Catholic indigenization. The Salish hymns, freely sung in the light of day, and indigenous ceremonies, driven into the recesses of a dark and muted underground, both contributed to a sense of collective indigeneity. Ultimately, this process of indigenization—of cultural integration, negotiation, and reinterpretation—could not be quelled. Nevertheless, the Jesuits found success. Unlike missionaries of other faiths who had abandoned their efforts, were driven from the Plateau, or were killed (Josephy 1965:252), the measured tolerance employed by the Jesuits ensured longevity and allowed for evolution and growth. What DeSmet could not have known as he set out west on the Oregon Trail in 1840 was that the path to Catholic indigenization had been laid a century before, when the Blackrobes first arrived within the vision of a Coeur d'Alene prophet. Unlike so many Native American peoples ambushed by Christian crusaders, the Coeur d'Alene were waiting for DeSmet and his religion, the answer to a promise borne through prophecy.

Indigeneity

Having invoked the terms *indigenization* and *indigeneity* as they relate to encounters between Jesuits and Native inhabitants of the Columbia Plateau region, I feel it is important to trace etymological lines that have shaped, and fairly recently reshaped, the terms' meaning. The origins of *indigenous* and its derivatives *(indigeneity, indigenization, indigenism)* stem from the Latin word *indigena*. Translated as "a native," the term first appeared in English in a 1598 document as a way to distinguish between cultural Others in a new America, between native "indigenes" and African slaves delivered to its shores (Cadena and Starn 2007:4).

From the beginning, the word was used by outside entities to refer to those already there—by colonizers to identify those being colonized. But while it is a word historically bound to colonial hegemony, "a concept framed by the Conquest" (McIntosh 2002:23), in the second half of the twentieth century indigenous peoples around the world began to own it, responding to the colonial legacy with a unified voice rooted in shared experience. Their stories were similar: loss of culture, loss of land, poverty, and an ongoing struggle to maintain identity. For centuries, colonial powers had delivered to indigenous peoples a lethal mix of programmatic acculturation on the one hand and systematic neglect on the other. What has been termed the "global indigenous movement" can be seen as a worldwide effort to decolonize, to turn back the lingering effects of colonialism while standing against current forces of conquest, whether led by a nation, a corporation, or some combination thereof.

The term *indigenous* circulates within local and global spheres, simultaneously informing identities both political and personal. The former sphere might consist a collective network framed in terms of the material, such as unending campaigns to wrestle land and natural resources back from states and state-sponsored corporations. The latter sphere deals with an immaterial sense of indigeneity, one that extends from the individual to others within a sheltered framework of cultural identity. While we are concerned primarily with indigeneity at a personal and local level, to not contend with the global/political implications of the term *indigenous* would be to ignore one end of a spectrum wholly dependent on the other.

While writing this introduction I came upon the following exchange via "Indigenous Peoples and Resources," a website providing daily updates on indigenous issues the world over. That day the site had a link to an interview conducted shortly after the United Nations Permanent Forum on Indigenous Issues released a report titled *State of the World's Indigenous Peoples*. The following is an exchange between the interviewer, Linda Mottram, and Vicki Tauli-Corpuz, chair of the UNPFII:

MOTTRAM: Indigenous peoples make up just five per cent of the global population. Yet they are about a third of the world's 900-million extreme poor, rural people. And in both developed and developing countries they suffer by every measure. A native American [*sic*] in the United States, for example, is 600 times more likely to contract tuberculosis and 62 per cent more likely to commit suicide than the general population. In Nepal the life expectancy gap is 20 years, while the report names projects in specific countries, including dam building in Malaysia and oil palm plantations in Indonesia, for contributing to the dispossession of indigenous peoples that's identified as a key issue contributing to their often grim lives. At the report's launch in New York, later posted on the UN's website, the chair of the UN Permanent Forum on Indigenous Issues, Vicki Tauli-Corpuz, said it was important that the document was the work of indigenous authors.

TAULI-CORPUZ: This is the first time that we would say people are not writing about us. We are writing about the current situation that we are living in different parts of the world.

(www.indigenouspeoplesissues.com, January 18, 2010)

Pointing to dispossession and disease as common factors in the ongoing struggle of indigenous peoples, Mottram's opening statement reflects the scope of the term *indigenous,* tying Native Americans and indigenous Nepalese, Malaysian, and Indonesian peoples together in a shared quest for justice and equal rights under the cross-cultural banner of indigeneity. It is a broad and inclusive use of the term that would have been unheard-of forty years ago. Tauli-Corpuz's response is also telling, expanding a conception initially reserved for First Peoples of the Americas into an indigenous "us," a community of 370 million indigenous peoples found throughout the world.[4]

This movement was necessitated by the global colonial legacy, during which the ravages of conquest produced similar patterns: violent oppression, subjugation, and survival followed by a reemergence and fight for human rights. While the shared collective experience of indigenous peoples is significant, at times the global movement threatens to eclipse the distinct cultural groups that constitute it, creating the perception of a unified homogenous whole rather than groups of people with their own unique histories, identities, and lifeways (Smith 1999:22). Local definitions become validated not within international forums or courts of law but within the closed circuit of cultural identity in indigenous communities. While an individual in the Columbia Plateau will recognize that he/she is indigenous, when asked, he/she will often self-identify through tribal and/or family affiliations: "I'm enrolled Nez Perce. My father is Nez Perce, my mother is Yakama"; or "I'm Spokan, my grandfather is Spokan, my grandmother is Coeur d'Alene and Salish." Native identity in the Plateau (and elsewhere) is localized, reflecting shared identities of those in one's family and community. Tracing family lineage pulls ancestral connections into the present, where individuals are living embodiments of the past. Indigeneity remains a distant concept, one that is of little consequence in this localized, day-to-day reality of being. One's sense of indigeneity is centered within the self—just as each individual is situated within a particular indigenous community. That community, in turn, is situated within a broader global community consisting of a network of peoples brought together by mirrored histories and contemporary struggles. The term *indigenous* covers this spectrum, and unlike a myriad of other words applied to cultural Others by popular authors, artists, or academics, *indigenous* has been embraced from the inside, a term utilized by First Peoples throughout the world to describe who they are: their identity, their experience, and their collective worldviews. As one localized story within a broader "indigenous studies series," *Songs of Power and Prayer in the Columbia Plateau* privileges firsthand accounts rooted in indigenous—or more succinctly, Native—ways of knowing. In the end, I hope it might contribute in its own way to the decolonization of Native peoples, largely through the voices of a medicine man and prayer leader and a Jesuit they considered one of their own.

Spirit and the Ethos of Indigeneity

Central to this story are oral histories of those closest to Mitch Michael and Gibson Eli, histories that reflect an indigenous worldview particular to Columbia Plateau people. By embracing these epistemologies, I am intentionally distancing this story from Western ways of knowing—epistemologies rooted in scientific methodologies employed within various disciplines in academic institutions (Smith 1999:65). The Western academy, having "constructed all the rules by which the indigenous world has been theorized," has amassed bodies of knowledge about Native peoples bereft of Native voices, voices that "have been overwhelmingly silenced" (Smith 1999:29). In countless ethnographies written from the outside looking in, Native realities such as spiritual power and the sacred have been relegated to the confines of "belief" and "superstition." From the point of European contact, within academia as well as the church, spiritual traditions of Native Americans have suffered derision and neglect, cast out in equal measure from the Ivory Tower and the Gates of Heaven.

For millennia, Native peoples of the Columbia Plateau region have cultivated a connection with the sacred. Through centuries of continual ceremony and prayer, the lines of demarcation between the spirit realm and the individual have dissolved, allowing the material and ethereal to meet in a shared continuum pregnant with the potential for exchange. Many of the recollections and oral histories contained herein—in particular, those in reference to Gibson Eli—take place within this spiritual continuum, a space within which Tom Connolly drifted into new understandings rooted in Native ways of knowing. Like the Jesuits who came before, Connolly benefited from a receptive congregation at the Sacred Heart mission in De Smet, Idaho. His experience, however, was quite different from that of his predecessors. In the same way the Catholic hymns were indigenized—absorbed, reconstructed, and re-sung—Connolly himself went through a process of indigenization, one that reshaped his theological perspective and worldview. He took cultural and spiritual cues from his "two grandfathers" and became a student of each, schooled in the ways of indigenous Columbia Plateau people. His role as an assistant to the medicine man led to a conversion of sorts, during which he broke with his Jesuit antecedents on long-held positions and critical issues, embracing aspects of indigenous ontologies previously discouraged and disdained. Michael and Eli escorted him into this ethos of indigeneity, a place where the technology of song had been honed and perfected over time, becoming a sacred tool capable of bending the laws of the familiar physical plane.

1

Power and Prophecy in the Plateau

Among religious prophetic traditions, found at the roots of many faiths throughout the world, indigenous Plateau prophecy stands out for one reason in particular: its reliance on song to relay its message and bring forth its power. Long before the influx of settlers and well into the postcontact period in the Plateau, many prophets were engaged in the visionary process, communicating with the realm of spirit through death and dreams, bringing songs, dances, and teachings back for the benefit of the People. Those who fell within the scope of the historical record—whether as perceived antagonists of the U.S. military or through oral accounts given to subsequent researchers—became a source of considerable attention in Plateau scholarship and popular history. Spiritual leaders, medicine people, and seers were anointed "prophets" by those eager to describe, and at times denigrate, practices for which they had little frame of reference. What is lost in these often biased and ethnocentric accounts is a sense of the depth of indigenous Plateau spiritual traditions. While participating in a dialogic refined over many centuries, prophets of the Plateau were engaged in a vibrant spiritual continuum with origins buried far beyond the reach of the historical eye, having their own sets of practices and terms for phenomena related to spiritual experience.

Consistent with other prophetic traditions, both within and beyond North America, increased visionary activity documented during the mid to late nineteenth century in the Plateau was accompanied by considerable upheaval and chaos.[1] Indigenous Plateau people suffered catastrophic losses in the face of Euro-American disease, beginning with a smallpox epidemic near the end of the eighteenth century (Miller 1985:33–35), the crest of a devastating wave that would swell to monstrous proportions with the successive stampede of settlers from the east. In addition, traditional lifeways were threatened by wars with the

U.S. government and its subsequent dictates on the one hand and intense missionary proselytizing on the other. Work among anthropologists, who have produced the bulk of the research on this period, has been focused on studies of acculturation and attendant deprivation. The visionary experience, and the role of song as an embodiment of that experience, has often been overlooked in such studies, viewed as an inconsequential artifact of cultural expression tied to external forces. Moreover, despite faithful documentation of accounts of visions and prophecies, prophets have often been approached with condescension, skepticism, or outright contempt. Researchers, unable to bridge the chasm between radically divergent, culturally conditioned worldviews, at times have gone out of their way to discredit prophecies. Clifford Trafzer, a longtime Plateau historian, offers possible reasons for the reluctance of researchers to understand indigenous spiritual traditions in North America and for their tendentious vilification of prophets:

> To many scholars the Indian world is foreign and
> uncompromising, sometimes even hostile, and too alien to
> relate to the fundamental tenets of Judeo-Christian religions
> to allow them to understand Native American religious
> concepts. Prophetic dreams, animal spirits, ceremonial songs,
> and various tribal spiritual dimensions were incomprehensible
> to academics, who operated from an intellectual methodology
> based on a different reality. . . . If native religions held little
> credence among most intellectuals, Indian prophets had
> even less credibility. . . . Often, American Indian prophets
> belied the intellectual framework employed by scholars who
> failed—or refused—to perceive correctly the preeminent role
> of these individuals in the Indian communities. And since a
> preponderance of the documentary evidence about Indian
> prophets has been written by whites who held holy men and
> women in contempt, it was easy for historians to neglect the
> significance of Indian prophets in the historical development
> of Indian-white relations. In fact, the task was made easier

since scholars could overlook or completely discount Indian oral sources or records written by individuals who knew and understood the people. (1986:x)

In approaching song as the embodiment of prophecy and catalyst for spiritual power, I dispense with ineffective "intellectual methodologies" and accept the reality of visionary experience by resituating indigenous ontologies within the framework of academic scholarship. There is a gaping hole in Native American scholarship where indigenous spirituality is concerned. To minimize or disregard spiritual experience within Native cultures, as so many cultural outsiders have, is to deny the very lifeblood of the People, the heart center from which everything else is fed. What is sorely needed is a paradigmatic shift in approach, away from a reality constructed and perpetuated by the Western academy to an indigenous spiritual reality—one that is no less real, even if the West's research tools are unable to grasp it. The general suspicion of Native spiritual practice held by early researchers and carried through to the present rings hollow in the face of countless accounts of prophetic experience that amount, in their totality, to an undeniable truth of indigenous spiritual experience.

The following accounts, while providing a sense of an embedded and recurring cultural phenomenon rooted in such experience, are typical in their dependence on song to realize and communicate the content of a prophecy. Although transcribed by non-Native researchers, all the accounts were drawn directly from Native individuals relaying oral histories. Still, in one of the accounts a researcher's bias clearly intrudes: Account 4 describes Smohalla as "semidelirious," implying that his experience may have been, at least in part, illusory. Reducing the experiences of individuals in such accounts to simple exhaustion, bereavement, or some sort of unconscious hallucinatory state reveals the cultural and academic conditioning of the researcher. However subtle such intrusions may seem, they have been immensely damaging, insidiously undermining and invalidating indigenous epistemologies shaped through centuries of spiritual praxis, where what may now be considered unbelievable was commonplace. The following accounts establish a foundation for future chapters, in which the phenomenology of song and power is freely explored within an epistemological framework distinctly Native in scope and design.

Account 1

The pom-pom comes from dreams.[2] A man called Luls lived at Mackay Creek on Umatilla reservation. In his dreams he saw he should have six drums. He died before 1870. In his dreams he saw a lot of people coming down in the clouds as though they were standing on them. They were all fixed up nice and clean with feathers in their hair. Their faces and hands were painted red. When he woke up from his sleep dreaming he saw his dream before him all the time. People talked to him and he didn't want to answer. He just wanted to think about what he saw in his dream. He was that way for maybe two or three weeks. He began singing what he had heard these people singing with their drums. His own family helped him. He told them for the first time what he had seen in his dream. He felt sad. He said, "I saw the holy people in my dream. They almost came down to this ground where we live. They are singing this song with drums and they told me to do these things on the holy day. Clean yourselves well on the Sabbath day and be ready to do these things." So they sang the song keeping time with their right arm [flexed upward at elbow]. He told the people, "You must not think anything bad against your friends. You must not think of things in this world. Think about what I say, of the beautiful people who almost came down to this world. They said they came from the holy country where our fathers, our children, and our friends go when they die. If we do this, keep ourselves clean in our hearts, and be kind to each other, we shall go to the same place as our dead relatives." (Allen Padawa in Dubois 1938:12)

The following account concerns Wiskaynatónmay, a Niimiipuu prophetess active in the Plateau between 1860 and 1870.

Account 2

People got their songs from being dead. When they would die they would get the song and come back to life with it. They don't come back to tell us what they heard now, because they embalm them. The people hear the songs but they can't get back. We used to keep them for three or four days, and lots of them would revive and give us songs. My mother's aunt was one of the last that got a song that way. My mother said that she saw the people all dressed up in buckskin and feathers standing on the clouds. They were all singing the song she brought back. There weren't any white people up there. She was going down this trail toward the people, and she came to a forks [*sic*] in the trail. There was a voice under a light that followed her and directed her. It told her to turn right and she did, but after she got down the road, the voice told her to stop, not to go any further. It told her to turn around. She did, and that was when she came back to life. In the old days when a person came back to life like that the people respected them. They would gather around and listen to the songs the person got. They would listen to what the person had seen and heard. (Walker 1985:50–51)

The following account tells of a vision and song given to the Umatilla prophetess Hununwe.

Account 3

Just before the allotments were given out, Hununwe died and came to. She told about the same things as Smoholla and Luls. She used to say at meeting, "I saw lots of people in the holy place. They told me to do these things, so I am doing this for a few days. (She meant thereby a few years.) Then I shall die

again and live with these holy people." A vision like this makes
a person head preacher. She used to sing a song which meant,
"They are having a joyous time and it is light for them but
we don't hear them unless we join in with them." Everyone
used lots of red and yellow paint in Hununwe's dance. (Allen
Padawa in Dubois 1938:14; parentheses in original).

Account 4
After days of fasting and abstinence from water atop the
mountains, Smowhala grew semidelirious. Every rustle of the
wind or chirp of a bird spoke to him in the language of the
preternatural. He fell asleep, the sleep of the dead; but, because
he was gifted, he awoke with a new song, a greater power,
and instructions to add new rituals to the fragments of an old
religion that had persisted through the dim years. (Relander
1956:70)

After the passing of his wife and child, during a period of intense
mourning, Jake Hunt, the founder of the Feather Religion, had a vision.

Account 5
A reliable convert at Yakima said that Jake was lying outside of
his house when he heard a voice command him to stop grieving
and to take up a new work. A song was received at this time.
Jake arose still in a trance state and went to the cemetery
dancing and singing his new song. His relatives, thinking he
had lost his mind, seized him and dragged him to the house.
There he recovered from his trance and accused his relatives of
having destroyed the full development of his powers. (Dubois
1938:24)

These accounts amount to a small sampling of prophetic visionary
experience in the Plateau in the nineteenth century. Many more
prophecies were documented and other prophets named, but we may

safely assume that countless others slipped past the historical lens, which was often focused on those viewed as a direct threat to colonial interests, such as the Wanapum prophet Smoholla.[3] The centrality of song within prophetic visionary experience is not unique to the accounts listed here, nor was it unique to indigenous Plateau groups in general; indeed, song can be found as an integral component of prophetic experience throughout indigenous North America. While song remains central, the details that surround the phenomenology of song transmission in the foregoing accounts vary in significant ways. Luls's experience, during which teachings and songs were given, was realized within a dream.[4] Wiskaynatónmay and Hununwe had their vision experience subsequent to their deaths.[5] Smoholla experienced his vision within the ceremonial sphere, while Jake Hunt had his visionary encounter while grieving the loss of his wife and child. This demonstrates that an individual may have a prophetic or visionary experience in various contexts, whether seeking such an experience or unwittingly falling into one: an important factor to consider as we revisit the phenomenon in subsequent chapters.

The Merging of Individual and Spirit

Rather than a one-way process, the visionary experience is an interdependent dialogic between the individual and the spirit realm, a mutually mediated spiritual continuum reflected in the use of song. Account 3 tells of a song sung by Hununwe that includes the dictum "we don't hear them unless we join in with them." In each of the cases listed above, the songs originated in the realm of spirit but did not become viable until actualized through the body and breath of the individual, sung for personal strength or the benefit of the People. At that moment the individual or group and the spirit realm are two parts of a dynamic whole, at the center of which sits the song—the very thing that binds them. To "hear" the spirit realm, to actualize power in a shared space, the individual or members of the collective group must merge with the realm of spirit, to sing the song "with them."[6] It might be said that prophets in the Plateau during the nineteenth century and the spirits that guided them were working together in this way to realize a common goal: a return to precontact stability in the face of rapid change. The use of song as an embodiment of the prophetic experience did not begin in the chaos of the postcontact era, however, but permeated the spiritual life of indigenous Americans long before the curious and covetous Other would stumble into the so-called New World. While these headlong explorers knew not where they were going or when they might get there, the prophets foretold their arrival.

Tawis Waikt

In a series of interviews conducted by Loran Olsen in 1970 and 1971, Sol Webb (Niimiipuu) sang and discussed songs that embodied prophecy. As a boy his grandfather, Weptestema'na', was present at a dance run by Tawis Waikt, a prophet who shared visions of dramatic events to come. Relaying what he had learned from his grandfather, Webb states, "He had this dream, or something. His name was Tawis Waikt. And he used to sing that song. Young girls used to dance around him" (Olsen 1974:5–6). Quoting Tawis Waikt, Webb continues, "My spirit tells me that this earth is going to be turned over, and the *koq álx* (buffalo or cattle) is going to be all over this country, and there will be no more vacant land as there is today" (Olsen and Webb 1972:3).

Webb states that the prophecy of Tawis Waikt occurred "over one hundred and fifty years ago," placing it in the 1820s or earlier. By that time, Lewis and Clark had made their way through the Columbia Plateau, but the area had not yet seen the influx of settlers in the decades following missionary activity in the mid-1830s. According to Webb's grandfather, at the time of Tawis Waikt's prophecy, some were incredulous: "And they said—well, alotta people, lotta those Indians says, 'Oh, he's crazy. How are those buffalos going to come here, when they all over in Montana . . . Who's gonna live . . . how they gonna live all over this country?' And my grandfather used to say 'They could see it now!' And it's true, he was right" (Olsen interview, 1970).

The foregoing demonstrates that for many during the time such impending changes were inconceivable. One can imagine that for the Niimiipuu, who had occupied lands that had remained intact and unmolested for as long as there had *been* Niimiipuu, the idea of the land being "turned over" must have seemed impossible. One of Tawis Waikt's songs from this period can be translated as "Me also, the earth says—continually you force me by your laws" (Olsen and Webb 1972:3). Evident in the translation is a concept that would have been foreign to the indigenous Plateau worldview: the earth being "forced." Exploitation of the earth, in any form, would have been offensive to Native Plateau people, who cultivated a symbiotic balance that required that one walk lightly and take only what was needed. Any thought of "forcing" or turning the earth over would have been viewed as counterintuitive and antithetical to long-term sustainability and survival. What could possibly be gained from turning the earth over, the soil of which held foods and fed the animals necessary for survival? How could so many people flood such a vast terrain? Many other prophecy songs from the Plateau spoke of impending ecological trauma. In an interview with the Niimiipuu Many Wounds, Lucullus McWhorter recorded words to prophecy songs that are among the most specific ever documented in the Plateau. Before singing for McWhorter, Many Wounds said, "Centuries before the advent of whites in our country, the Nez Perces had warnings of what was coming, revealed by their prophets, through Dream Songs. We still remember those songs, handed down through the generations." In McWhorter's account, Many Wounds translated one such song as "All people, and animals! Creation as existing to be overthrown, destroyed! Buffalos exterminated! Elk and deer fenced, confined. Eagles caged from flying! Indians confined to narrowed bodies of land. Liberty and happiness broken and shortened." Another song spoke of the exploitation of natural resources: "Rough places, crooked places of Nature's beauty, some one will smooth and straighten. Flowers looking upward will no longer bloom. Forests will melt away, game disappearing. Rivers to be held back and lessened. Salmon no longer plentiful for the tribes" (McWhorter 1952:83–84).

Today, a simple drive through the Columbia Plateau reveals prophecies foretold within the songs of a precontact indigenous era. Forests have given way to agriculture consisting of foreign mono-crops (primarily wheat) covering vast swaths of southeastern Washington, northeastern Oregon, and north-central Idaho, an area referred to as the Palouse (named, ironically, for the Palúus, an indigenous group driven from most of their ancestral homelands). For miles, one can look out over the region and see gently rolling hills made "smooth" and "straightened"—empty, uniform, and bereft of native trees and flora (as well as the native people) that once took root there. Rivers throughout the Columbia Plateau have been "held back and lessened" by a multitude of dams, devastating salmon runs and irreparably damaging the lifeways of Columbia Plateau people.[7] And while the dams and farms led to tremendous economic expansion for Euro-Americans in the region, indigenous territories were being "narrowed," first by reservation boundaries and then under the Dawes Act of 1887.[8]

"Book" Prophecies

In addition to impending ecological trauma at the hands of whites, prophets of the Plateau predicted the suffering that would accompany the arrival of a book in the hands of missionaries: "Soon there will come from the rising sun a different kind of man from any you have yet seen, who will bring with them a book and will teach you everything, and after that the world will fall to pieces" (Wilkes 1845:4:467).

The foregoing prophecy was relayed to Charles Wilkes of the U.S. Exploring Expedition in 1841 by Silimxnotylmilakabok, one of the leaders of the Spokan tribe. Also known by the names Cornelius and Bighead, he shared the prophecy delivered by a Spokan medicine man some fifty years prior, placing its occurrence at the end of the eighteenth century.[9] This preceded the appearance of Lewis and Clark in the Plateau and occurred well before the "book," or Bible, would arrive.[10]

Columbia Plateau scholars have focused on three potential sources for Christian influence prior to the arrival of missionaries in the 1830s: trapper-explorer David Thompson, who entered the Columbia Plateau in 1807 not long after Lewis and Clark; Kutenai Pelly and Spokan Garry, indigenous Plateau children sent to the Red River mission school north of Minnesota in 1825 to receive formal Christian training; and

Old Ignace, an Iroquois who along with members of his band left the Catholic mission at Caughnawaga (in present-day Quebec) in 1812 and settled among the Salish in Montana by 1820 (Miller 1985:52–53). While Thompson was identified as a practicing Christian, the general consensus is that his role in spreading Christian doctrine was inconsequential, and more likely nonexistent. Upon their return from the Red River school, Kutenai Pelly and Spokan Garry apparently had little influence in spreading Christianity. As a leader of his tribe, Spokan Garry no doubt carried some influence, but Protestant and Catholic missionaries, soon to enter the scene, would prove much more influential.[11] Old Ignace's role in Christian diffusion has generally been given primacy in speculation surrounding premissionary Christian influence in the Plateau. Early Catholic sources credit Old Ignace with introducing elements of Catholicism to his "adopted brethren" within the Salish tribe as early as 1820 (Palladino 1922:8; Bischoff 1945:9). However, in *Prophetic Worlds: Indians and Whites on the Columbia Plateau*, Christopher Miller makes a compelling case for interest among Columbia Plateau tribes in Christianity before it manifested physically, whether through the teachings of Old Ignace or through missionaries over a decade later. In Miller's view, Thompson, Pelly, Garry, and Old Ignace represented to Plateau people the eventual fulfillment of prophecies, indicative of a spiritual continuum that was not as susceptible to external influence as many have maintained. Interest among Columbia Plateau tribes in Christianity was rooted in longstanding and established internal spiritual processes necessary to validate elements before they were brought into the fold of indigenous spiritual practice and ceremony. In the same manner that songs and prophecies were transmitted to individuals before contact with Euro-Americans, so too were the elements of the religion that would accompany them. It would not have been enough to hand over a book and cajole or threaten. Initially, Christianity did not emanate from churches that dotted the landscape in the Columbia Plateau in the 1840s; it was drawn from a spiritual landscape visited by the singing, the dancing, the dreaming, and the dead. It came not from the pulpit or pew but through visions of those tapping into a spiritual continuum that was fluid and open to change. The "Nez Perce–Flathead" delegation in 1831 was fundamentally motivated by numerous prehistoric prophecies that spoke of teachings, knowledge, and power that would accompany the "black robes" and the "Sabbath book" (Olsen 1974:5).

Elizabeth Wilson, a Niimiipuu singer, was recorded in 1966 singing a prophecy song listed by the recorder as "Ipnú·cilí·lpt."[12] Translated as "turning," *ipnú·cilí·lpt* refers to circular dancing around an axis (Walker 1985:34; Aoki 1994:1255). While translating the song, Wilson speaks of a prophetic process that predated Euro-American contact:

> You don't know your record, what's wrote about your life, your soul, in the book. So they didn't know what the book was but whoever visioned must have seen [the] book and where things were wrote. *Tí·mes*. They didn't know, Indians, before white people what *tí·mes* was, No! But still they had this already prophesized through vision. So you can't doubt there is real something up in heaven that is used to help Indians because they didn't have any bible or anything. That's what it means, *tí·mes*, "bible." . . . Bible means *tí·mes* too. (Olsen interview, 1971)

Sometime before contact, Shining Shirt of the Upper Pend Oreille had a vision of strangers from the east. Jacqueline Peterson states, "He prophesied the coming of fair-skinned men wearing long black robes who would teach the Indians a new way of praying and new moral law. The Black Robes would bring peace, he predicted, but their arrival would also mean the beginning of the end of all the people who then inhabited the land" (Peterson and Peers 1993:20).

The Prophecy of Circling Raven

Oral history maintains that Circling Raven was the primary leader of the Coeur d'Alene from 1660 to 1760, one hundred years during which he cultivated loyalty through a blend of insight and wisdom.

Also recognized as a powerful prophet, he was possessed of the ability to shepherd the Coeur d'Alene people into a future foretold through the raspy exhorts of his invaluable *sumesh*,[13] the raven. In 1740, while hunting buffalo within lands that belonged to the Crow and Blackfeet,

> Circling Raven began singing his prophecy songs, and he told his people to listen for three ravens that were coming to give them news. In just a few minutes, three ravens circled the encampment and gave out three calls. Circling Raven asked the people if they understood. His people told him: "No, we don't understand birds." Circling Raven told the people what the ravens had said: "You have enemies who have already spied you out. They are already preparing for an attack, therefore prepare yourselves." This is how the Coeur d'Alene chief of those days gained his name. (Seltice 1990:14–16)

After the buffalo hunt, the Coeur d'Alene set out for their permanent winter camp in what is now known as Kingston, Idaho. According to the oral record, Circling Raven conducted a medicine dance that year, fulfilling a vision experienced some twenty years prior in which he had been told of Jesus and his resurrection (Ibid.). During the same ceremony, Circling Raven shared a prophecy in which "men in Blackrobes" would one day appear on the horizon, armed with little more than "crossed sticks," new words, and powerful medicines to help the People (Fortier 2002:30–31). For decades, Circling Raven anxiously sought the Blackrobes, but as he entered his final years he accepted that the eyes he had been granted in life would not in the end behold them (Seltice 1990:18). He assembled his People and recounted his visions one last time, reminding them that the fulfillment of his prophecies offered protection in a world that would soon see dramatic changes.

Before his death in 1760 he asked his son, Twisted Earth, to look after his prophecy as well as the People (Fortier 2002:30). Every summer thereafter, Twisted Earth traveled to the valley of the Salish in search of the Blackrobes. Some twenty years later news arrived, in a form familiar to his father. In preparation for the medicine dance of that year Twisted Earth told his people to hang poles at each end of the twelve- by twenty-foot lodge. Once the dance began, a raven and crow arrived, flying in through a hole at the top of the lodge and settling upon one of the poles. To honor the presence of the winged messengers, the people began to sing their prophecy songs. After some time the birds let out a series of caws and took flight, following the line of smoke from the three fires, flying out of the lodge and disappearing into darkness. They told Twisted Earth it would be sixty years before the Blackrobes would enter the Plateau, so he should be patient and continue the medicine dance. They added that it was pleasing to the Creator, who had come to earth as a baby many years before (Seltice 1990:18).

The prophets of the Plateau featured in the foregoing paragraphs participated in a tradition formed through centuries of direct encounters with the spirit realm. Such encounters provided a window through which prophets of the eighteenth and nineteenth centuries in the Plateau could gaze into a largely unrecognizable future, bringing inconceivable changes that would dramatically reshape their world. Prophecies of this time served as an early warning system, and the extent to which the people rallied—by actively bringing a vision to fruition—determined their ability not only to meet impending changes but also to survive. The fulfillment of a prophecy was often dependent on song, carried by the voices of the prophet as well as the People, sustaining and nurturing a vision from its origin to its end. Song was power; song was prayer; and within communities where the presence of the spirit realm was pervasive, song was ever-present. The centrality of song among the Coeur d'Alene was not lost on a Blackrobe by the name of Pierre-Jean DeSmet, who sought to instill within indigenous Columbia Plateau people the words of a foreign prophet, one who lived and died a world away.

2

Christians Answer the Call

Upon his arrival in Coeur d'Alene country in April 1842, Fr. Pierre-Jean DeSmet was escorted to the lodge of Twisted Earth. The air within the lodge hung heavy. It had been one hundred years since Circling Raven's vision, and there before Twisted Earth sat the fulfillment of a prophecy. After a period of prolonged and quiet contemplation, Twisted Earth spoke:

> My father looked for you for a long time. Many times he
> searched the entire Bitterroot Valley, and many times he
> went beyond the divide. Finally at an old age, he asked me
> to continue the search for the Black Robe. It has been fully a
> hundred years since my father first sang the prophecy songs of
> the "coming of the Black Robe." When he died, I continued
> to watch for the Black Robe. Now it has been eighty years
> of crossing the mountains, looking throughout the Bitterroot
> Valley and following my father's footsteps many times beyond
> the divide. I had full tribal backing during enemy attacks north
> and south of the divide. We spared no valley, no plain, and we
> crossed every mountain to fulfill my father's prophecy. Today
> that prophecy has been fulfilled! I thank the Great Spirit in
> prayers that I will say the rest of my life, not just in words,
> but from my heart as I embrace this fulfillment of my devoted
> eighty-year search. I am listening, together with all my children
> scattered throughout the valley, along the St. Joe and the
> Coeur d'Alene Rivers, and a number of families at the head
> of this lake. Had they known that my father's prophecy was
> going to be fulfilled today, they would all be here to give you
> a reception. They all wished to see this day, as did I, and my
> father before me. We have been disliked at times for seeking the

Christian Faith, disliked at times for not accepting the faith of one who rambled on and on, disliked at times for trespassing in trying to find the Black Robe. But now, let us hear you! (Seltice 1990:33)

By DeSmet's own account, the People wasted little time in providing that reception: "The tidings of my coming soon spread through all the country. The Indians were to be seen flocking from all sides, through forest and plain, by the rivers and the great lake, to meet me, and hear the word of God from the very lips of the Black Gown. My visit, consequently, had the most beneficial results. I baptized all the little children in the tribe and a good number of adults, who had hastened with holy avidity to come and receive the mustard seed mentioned in the Gospel" (DeSmet 1985:26).

Although DeSmet hit the ground running, he was somewhat late to the game. Methodists, Protestants, and Congregationalists beat Fr. Pierre DeSmet to the punch in efforts to Christianize the Plateau, building missions years before DeSmet would see the walls of the first Catholic mission erected in 1841. Nevertheless, he had a distinct advantage. Not only was he viewed among many of the Coeur d'Alene as the fulfillment of Circling Raven's prophecy, he benefited from centuries of missionary experience within the Roman Catholic Church. Spurred by the Council of Trent in 1545 and aided by the expansion of the Portuguese and Spanish colonial enterprise, the Catholic Church dramatically extended its reach during the Counter-Reformation.[1] Drawing inspiration from earlier religious orders such as the Franciscans and Dominicans, the Society of Jesus (founded in 1540 by the Basque nobleman Ignatius Loyola) represented a growing undercurrent within a sweeping sea change. In addition to reasserting religious dominance, the Church was experiencing a period of spiritual renewal during which the Jesuits swelled in ranks, filtering out into Africa, Asia, and the Americas (Brockey 2007:6–7). One such experiment in South America became known as the Jesuit Reductions in Paraguay.

The Reductions

The Guaraní,[2] numbering an estimated 150,000 at the point of contact with Europeans (Caraman 1976:34), provided the impetus and inspiration for the Reductions.[3] In the second decade of the sixteenth century, European explorers began trickling into Guaraní homelands. That trickle turned into a torrent after the construction of a Spanish settlement in 1537 that would later become known as Asunción.[4] Initially, members of various Christian religious orders who accompanied early explorers were preoccupied with their European constituents, leaving the Guaraní outside the scope of their Christian activities during the first few decades of the Spanish occupation. That changed with the arrival of the Franciscan Luis de Bolaños, who established eighteen Guaraní villages from 1580 to 1593 (1976:26). Just as critical as the villages to his missionary efforts were his texts, which included a grammar, a vocabulary, and a prayer book as well as catechisms in the Guaraní language.

Though the first Jesuits on the scene made use of the linguistic strands left by Bolaños to appeal to the Guaraní, their approach to the missionary process was quite different. After suffering through nearly seventy years of depravities at the hands of Spanish and Portuguese settlers who routinely sought to capture, enslave, and/or murder them, the Guaraní had become rightfully wary of Europeans.[5] For the Jesuits to be successful in their missionary enterprise, they recognized the need to keep the Guaraní out of the clutches of the European colonists and segregated from the settlements occupied by them. The missionaries found an important ally in the Spanish king. Concerned about the colonial competition of the Portuguese, low on funds, and struggling to control the larger Guaraní population within the framework of the slave trade, Philip III responded favorably to a Jesuit appeal, sending a letter to the Spanish governor of Asunción, Hernando de Saavedra, in 1609 outlining a strategy of nonviolent coercion. Hoping for eventual submission of the Indians, Philip III proposed that priests stand in for the military, marshaling the Guaraní into "reductions," a series of Catholic townships along the upper Paraná River in the province of

Guaíra, removed from Spanish settlements and free of local control (Gott 1993:28–29).[6] It was a great deal for the Jesuits. In an agreement fashioned between Saavedra and Fr. Diego de Torres, the Jesuit provincial in Paraguay, they would gain unfettered access to thousands of men, women, and children they sought to transform into fresh proselytes of the Catholic faith. An essential ingredient in that transformation would be song.

Although music was marginalized within the newly founded Society of Jesus, by the end of the sixteenth century Jesuit institutions had become primary hubs for the development of sacred music throughout Europe. The religious sensibilities of Jesuit missionaries dispatched to South America were formed within such institutions, virtually ensuring that music would be heard emanating from the missions of Paraguay in the early seventeenth century (Nawrot 2004:74). The full utility of music, however, would not become evident to the Jesuits until they began exploring the rivers utilized by Spanish and Portuguese explorers nearly a century before. Travelling by canoe, the Jesuits often joined one another in the singing of familiar Catholic hymns. Intrigued by these foreign songs of strangers, the Guaraní began emerging from the forests along the river's shore to absorb their odd melodies: just when all means to reach the Guaraní seemed to have been exhausted, the Jesuits stumbled upon a powerful lure. They immediately capitalized on the opportunity, adding instruments to their canoe excursions, weaving a musical web in which the Guaraní would soon be caught (Fülöp-Miller 1930:285). Song became their central strategy, and they wasted no time in exploiting its potential: "A Missionary could hardly begin singing some canticles relating Christian doctrine, but these savage infidels at that time would instantly bolt out from their thickets, and lurking holes, and follow with the greatest transports the voice they heard. When the Missionary perceived a great number gathered about him, he would then set out with preaching evangelical truths, thus prepare the way for founding a new *Reduction*" (Muratori 1759:87–88).

Drawing largely from accounts of the Paraguayan Reductions written by Cajetan Cattaneo, a Jesuit who arrived in Paraguay in 1729,

Lodovico Muratori—while reflecting the dehumanizing views held by the missionaries toward their indigenous "infidels"—emphasizes the importance of song in establishing a connection that had previously eluded them. Song served as nothing less than a foundation for Catholic conversion, and music remained integral to the formation of each new reduction.

Jesuits among the Guaraní were not the first to utilize music in the missions. In 1523, missionaries in Veracruz requested that any new recruits sent from Europe be able to play an instrument. In 1527, a Franciscan by the name of Pedro de Gant founded a school in Mexico centered on music education, and by 1528, Jodoco Ricke (also a Franciscan) had trained indigenous students to read and write music as well as play a variety of European instruments at a school in Quito (Caraman 1976:213). The Jesuits in Paraguay, however, took the concept much further than their missionary predecessors in South America, using music as an engine to drive a Catholic industry that, at its zenith, would consist of over thirty reductions comprising tens of thousands of indigenous converts.[7]

Teaching hymns in the Guaraní language constructed by Bolaños, Simón Maceta and José Cataldino, two of Paraguay's earliest Jesuit pioneers, assembled the Guaraní every morning for lessons in reading and singing.[8] They were following the dictate of Fr. Diego de Torres, who in 1610 further urged "that in each church an office of sacristan . . . be established and six to eight cantors selected who—through their singing—would magnify the brilliance with which every feast, Mass, Salve sung on Saturday, and Matins (*tinieblas*) should be observed" (Lozano in Nawrot 2004:74). In addition to training cantors and implementing a comprehensive catechesis consisting of songs interspersed with pictures, symbols, and dances (Caraman 1976:214), the Jesuits provided instruction in the performance of various stringed instruments, including the *vihuela de arco*, a guitar-like instrument popular in sixteenth-century Spain (Nawrot 2004:74). Before long, music pulsated continuously from the center of each new reduction, where "[a]lmost every function of everyday life was performed to the strains of music. As early as 5 A.M., the people were summoned by a fanfare of trumpets to church, where mass was celebrated with much singing, intoning of responses, and instrumental music, for the missionaries held that 'nothing was so conducive to inculcating in the Indians a reverence for God and love of his worship, or to make the Christian doctrines more easily understood by them, as their accompaniment by music'" (Fülöp-Miller 1930:286).

The missionaries soon realized, to their apparent surprise, that the Guaraní had an extraordinary aptitude for music. They noted that as the Guaraní command of songs grew, so did their instrumental fluency. While visiting San Ignacio Guazú (the first reduction) in 1634, Bernardino Cárdenes, then bishop of Asunción, commented on the "cleanness and neatness (*curiosidad*) of the churches and their altars" and the "careful attention paid to the divine cult, and worship, with music and songs, so able, so well rehearsed, with such a variety of instruments, that are worth of praise" (Hernández in Nawrot 2004:75). By the mid-seventeenth century, the Catholic Guaraní were adept at playing bells, organs, cornets, and trumpets. They were also constructing them, so well in fact that Sepp von Reinegg, an accomplished musician who joined the Jesuits in 1674, could not distinguish between two organs in his reduction church—one brought from Europe and the other fashioned from its likeness by Guaraní artisans (Nawrot 2004:76).

The musical legacy established within the reductions continued well beyond the expulsion of the Jesuits in 1767. For over 150 years, the Catholic Guaraní had excelled in the musical traditions of Europe, mastering a foreign musical language. The music did not remain foreign, however, but for those within the reductions quickly became an integral component of Guaraní indigenous identity, embodied and expressed long after the Jesuit voices in South America grew silent (Nawrot 2004:82–83). Inspired by what the Jesuits accomplished in Paraguay, Pierre DeSmet and his Jesuit companions sought to pick up where they left off with the founding of St. Mary's Mission among the Salish in September 1841.[9] With Muratori's account of the Jesuit reductions in hand (a book DeSmet referred to as "our Vade Mecum"), DeSmet and his fellow Jesuits found more than inspiration; they identified a model by which they intended to build their "empire of Christian Indians" in the interior Northwest (DeSmet 1905:306).

The Rocky Mountain Missions

It would not be easy. Among the Coeur d'Alene,[10] as well as other tribes, there were many who remained wary or ambivalent toward the Blackrobes and their religion. The space between Circling Raven's vision and DeSmet's arrival spanned a lifetime, and the prophetic words of Circling Raven had grown dim. The task of opening the new Mission of the Sacred Heart fell to Fr. Nicholas Point, who encountered resistance from leaders of the tribe from the outset, including Twisted Earth, who allegedly became disillusioned when the Jesuits did not build the Church of the Sacred Heart in his territory. To placate Twisted Earth (referring to him by his Salish moniker "Stella'am," a word meaning "thunder"), Nicholas Point and his fellow Jesuits agreed to spend their first winter among his band (Olsen interview, 1993; Point 1967:54, 56).

By Point's account, he and his companions were received enthusiastically, with Twisted Earth's "people flock[ing] around [them] to shake hands." He further claims that as a result of a First Friday of December ceremony, during which "the Coeur d'Alenes came respectfully to kiss" a tree that was erected to signify their "Redemption," gambling ceased among the Coeur d'Alene, as did "diabolical visions" and medicine dances. Any early success appears to have been short-lived, however, as the Blackrobes sowed seeds of doubt among their Native neophytes: "The Cross, instead of being a blessing for the fishermen and hunters, seemed to drive away the fish and animals, which in other years, had been so abundant." When Point concluded that these circumstances had contributed to a resurgence of Coeur d'Alene ceremonies, he took an aggressive stance, ensuring that "every day, medicine sacks, an animal's tail, a feather, or some similar object . . . were brought to the missionaries lodge and thrown into the fire" (Point 1967:67). Given the manner in which events unfolded among the Coeur d'Alene, it is not difficult to imagine Twisted Earth's animosity as deriving from much more than just the location of the Sacred Heart church. The perceived failure of the First Friday ceremony, followed by Point's attack on sacred Coeur d'Alene spiritual traditions, did little to instill confidence in the religion of the Blackrobes and undoubtedly caused Twisted Earth and others to question the Jesuits' methods as well as their religion's efficacy. Johnny Arlee, a cultural leader among the Salish, speaks of the consequences of the spiritual repression practiced by the Blackrobes as well as the squandering of the goodwill that awaited them upon their arrival:

> See, in the *beginning*—going back to Shining Shirt's vision— they already *knew* of the Blackrobes coming. So they were expecting this and when the news came to them from the Iroquois then they were *really* happy,[11] excited that Shining Shirt's vision was coming to pass, and so they sent their delegations. And with the Indian people in a circle and everything—their council in a circle, their leaders in a circle— the Blackrobe was *invited* into that circle. But he in turn *condemned* everybody in that circle and said everything that they did was *wrong*—practicing of the sweat lodges and all of this. It *split* that circle, *broke* that circle. He [DeSmet] had a lot of people believe this way and a lot of them didn't. The ones that didn't took their medicine bundles and held onto them. And that's what's alive today. (Olsen interview, November 24, 1990)

Virginia Matt (a daughter of Mitch and Mary Michael) discusses the efforts on the part of her grandfather—a well-respected leader of the Coeur d'Alene tribe—to preserve Indian traditions at risk under the repressive policies of the Blackrobes:

> The Blackrobes went and told the Indian people they would have to burn all their regalia. My grandpa Morris Antelope, he wouldn't. That was part of their life, you know, and why

Fr. Pierre DeSmet pictured with Native Columbia Plateau leaders at Ft. Vancouver in 1859. Wars between the U.S. government and Plateau tribes had ceased and DeSmet was taking tribal leaders on a "peace tour" organized by the government. Pictured in the back row, left to right: Chief Denis (Thunder's Robe), leader of the Colville; Bonaventure (Chinmitkasy), leader of the Coeur d'Alene; Fr. DeSmet; Francis Xavier (Saxa), Iroquois/Salish leader and son of Old Ignace. Pictured in the front row, left to right: Victor (Aldmaklen), leader of the lower Kalispel; Alexander (Canachkkstchin), also a leader of the Kalispel; Adolph (Squilsquilskape, Red Feather), leader of the Salish; and Andrew Seltice, then a recently appointed leader of the Coeur d'Alene. (De Smetiana Collection, Jesuit Missouri Province Archives, St. Louis IX-L2-A)

were they told to burn them up? They said, "If you're going to be a Catholic you can't have this, you can't War Dance." A lot of them burned their costumes, started going to church and learning to pray and all this. And I guess they went around from home to home to check to see if you got rid of your stuff and grandpa took his and put it upstairs and hid it between the boards. He put it all there and left it there. They didn't find it. (Hamill interview, July 23, 2009)

A painting by Fr. Nicholas Point depicting a vision quest in which a Native man is visited by spirit animals sent forth by the Devil. (AJC-GLC, BO-0043.2, Songe mystérieux.) This painting is reproduced in color between pages 50 and 51.

Another painting by Fr. Point appears to depict animal spirits in a different light. Within the scene, a medicine man (lower right corner) appeals to his animal spirit for help in a hunt. As a result, the hunt is successful. (AJC-GLC, BO-0043-19.1, Chasse aux cerfs.) This painting is reproduced in color between pages 50 and 51.

In this painting, Fr. Point depicts a medicine man before his spirit helper. While playing the flute the medicine man is met with rays of sunlight, a metaphor for divine inspiration that can be found in many of Point's paintings. (AJC-GLC, BO-0043-15.2, Le medecin.) This painting is reproduced in color between pages 50 and 51.

Earlier in its history the Society of Jesus was more culturally accommodating, taking a big tent approach to Christian conversion that represented an expansion of both mind and mission. This was particularly evident in Asia, where the Jesuits "were motivated by a firm belief in the universal applicability of Christian teaching and by a conviction that the Christian language had an elasticity that permitted it to conform to the contours of even the most widely disparate cultures" (Brockey 2007:6). The founders of the first China mission, Matteo Ricci and Michele Ruggieri, stretched the Christian language too far for the Dominicans and Franciscans in China, who were appalled at the Jesuits' efforts to accommodate the existing philosophical and religious systems of Confucianism, Buddhism, and Taoism. In the end the Dominicans and Franciscans prevailed, winning a protracted battle that would become known as the "Chinese Rites controversy." At the center of the controversy was the question as to what constituted worship. Offerings made to departed ancestors and the emperor during Confucian rites—

defined as political and secular acts by the Jesuits—were viewed by the Franciscans and Dominicans as worship, an act reserved for God alone. With a decree from Pope Clement XI, the period of cultural accommodation among the Jesuits, at least for the foreseeable future, had come to a close.[12] The first Jesuits in the Columbia Plateau would have felt compelled to abide by the restrictions set forth by the Church in the previous century, taking aim at the ceremonies, ceremonial objects, and animal spirits that pulled the focus of worship away from a singular Christian God.

Fortunate for DeSmet and Point, they had in their midst a number of dedicated Coeur d'Alene and Salish people willing to look past their doctrinal rigidity to the sacred Blackrobe prophecies of Circling Raven and Shining Shirt. Foremost among them was Louise Siuwhéem, one of the first adults on the shores of Coeur d'Alene Lake to receive baptism in the spring of 1842 (DeSmet 1985:26). As a direct descendant of Circling Raven with familial ties to other leaders of the Coeur d'Alene tribe, Siuwhéem was influential. DeSmet noted, "Before her Baptism, even, she was remarkable for her rare modesty and reserve, great gentleness, and solid judgment. Her words were everywhere listened to with admiration and pleasure, and her company sought in all families" (1985:25). Point remarked that Siuwhéem as well as her sister Martha, "who had been baptized among the first, were remarkable in more than one respect by reason of their virtue" (Point 1967:71).[13] Louise was steadfast and loyal to the priests and their cause, an intrepid "believer" with clout. Epitomizing the qualities the Jesuits sought to instill throughout the entire tribe, Siuwhéem became indispensable and was quickly appointed by Point to head teacher of the catechism (1967:37). She became a primary mediator, negotiating the space between Catholicism and indigeneity, going where Jesuits were unable to tread and transforming Catholic doctrine into something her people could recognize and embody.

To the delight of DeSmet and Point (as well as Frs. Joset and Gazzoli, their immediate successors), she boldly pursued unbaptized holdouts within the tribe, including powerful medicine men both revered and feared. In addition, she took dozens of children into her home for extended periods of religious instruction and acted as a nurse to those with various ailments, earning her the title of "good grandmother" among her people (Seltice 1990:54). In writings dedicated to her accomplishments, DeSmet credits her with nothing less than achieving "a complete and blessed change of the whole tribe" (1985:39). What is perhaps most compelling, however, is how Siuwhéem went about her work, much of which remained out of sight of her Jesuit teachers. For instance, DeSmet was surprised to learn that

> [f]or a long time she went regularly to the missionaries cabin to ask explanations and instructions on the Holy Sacrament of the altar, without his [Fr. Greg Gazzoli] supposing it to result from any motive but a desire of instruction. It was not until after the death of Louise, that he learned that when she had fully comprehended the meaning and seen the explanation of the principal ceremonies and rubrics in the celebration of the most holy mystery, she composed short prayers, full of unction, like those found in our best prayer books. I must remark here that this practice was then as yet unknown by the catechumens among the Indians, for the missionaries, especially in the first years that followed the establishment of the mission, were unable to go beyond the most elementary instructions on the points of doctrine of the most absolute necessity. (DeSmet 1985:48)

For Siuwhéem, it was necessary to "go beyond" the efforts of missionaries, who were unfamiliar with the Coeur d'Alene dialect and therefore incapable of transmitting the nuances of their faith. In a letter dated June 21, 1859—a full seventeen years after the first Coeur d'Alene mission was established,[14] and six years after Siuwhéem's passing—Fr. Joseph Joset relayed the continued struggle among Jesuits in contending with the Coeur d'Alene language: "The language is the greatest difficulty. One must learn it the best he can. There is no written language, there are no interpreters, there is very little analogy with other tongues. The pronunciation is very harsh, the turn of thought is entirely different from ours. My catechist remarked to me the other day, 'You pronounce like a child learning to talk . . .'" (DeSmet 1985:65).

In addition to filling in gaps lost in translation, Siuwhéem created a subtext by which she absorbed Catholicism into the fold of a collective indigenous worldview, using tools available to the Coeur d'Alene people before Circling Raven's vision and the arrival of the Blackrobes. Moving well beyond the doctrine prescribed, she went where the Jesuits were unwilling (and unable) to tread, entering the spiritual continuum and encountering spirits of those who had passed. Attributing it to "her great devotion for the souls in purgatory," DeSmet writes that "[e]very day, even during the rigorous season, she proceeded to the cemetery to spend some time there in prayer. When the household occupations of her poor family prevented her visiting it by day, she went there late in the evening, or even during the night. This was frequently the case. . . . [S]everal times it happened that when at prayer in the cemetery she would be seized with affright, at the sight of fantastic figures that she seemed to behold before her" (1985:49).

In addition to interacting with spirits in a manner cultivated by her ancestors, Siuwhéem engaged in "long prayers and frequent fasts" (DeSmet 1985:34), displaying a spiritual fortitude rooted in indigenous praxis. Unlike the Jesuits who counseled her, she understood that Catholic conversion would succeed only to the extent that it conformed to the spiritual sensibilities and epistemologies of the Coeur d'Alene. Toward this end, she not only indigenized the Catholic faith through the creation of prayers in Salish, she likewise translated and taught hymns in Salish, hymns such as "Sacred Heart, I Am Your Soldier," "Jesus, Have Mercy," and "Oh, If I Could Fly" (Seltice 1990:54). Louise Siuwhéem was acutely aware, in a way that Jesuits at the Mission of the Sacred Heart only vaguely understood, that for Catholicism to be embodied by the Coeur d'Alene people, it would first need to be sung.

3

The Old Indian Hymns

Like the Jesuits in Paraguay, the first Blackrobes in the Columbia Plateau viewed hymns translated into Salish as lures to draw in converts who, through the pedagogy and protocols of their reductions, might be plucked from the dark recesses of their own "savage" souls. Upon entering Salish country for the first time in July 1840, DeSmet was surprised to learn they had "hymns" of their own:

> I made known to them my conversation with their chiefs,
> the plan which I meant to follow for their instruction, and
> the necessary frame of mind that the Great Spirit required of
> them to comprehend and practice the holy law of Jesus Christ,
> who alone could save them from the torment of hell, make
> them happy on earth and procure them after this life eternal
> happiness with God in heaven. After that I said the evening
> prayers, and finally they sang together, in a harmony which
> surprised me very much, and which I thought admirable for
> savages, several songs of their own composition, on the praise
> of God.[1] It would be impossible to describe to you the emotions
> that I felt at this moment. How touching it is for a missionary
> to hear the benefactions of the Most High proclaimed by poor
> children of the forests, who have not yet had the happiness of
> receiving the light of the gospel! (DeSmet 1905:224–25)

It is safe to assume that DeSmet's delight at hearing the Salish songs was attributable, in large measure, to what he viewed as the Salish people's predisposition toward singing. In addition to displaying an "admirable" level of musical acuity, DeSmet observed their use of song as a primary vehicle for spiritual expression. The Jesuits would ask them to use Catholic hymns the same way; and if all went as planned, songs written in "the light of the gospel" would drown out the pre-Christian songs of their Plateau congregations, rendering them at once invisible and obsolete.

Even while struggling to grasp the basics of a complex language, Frs. Point, Mengarini, and DeSmet set about translating liturgical songs into Salish. In addition to their pedagogical role alongside reading, writing, and arithmetic at St. Mary's (Olsen and Connolly 2001:13), hymns were employed by the Jesuits of the first Rocky Mountain mission to imbue the Salish with a sense of Catholicism the missionaries hoped would inhabit their souls. Inspired by the "method employed by our Fathers of Paraguay to improve the minds and hearts of their neophytes," DeSmet established rules that would guide the missions, including prescribed methods for the administration of "the sacraments, singing, music, etc" (DeSmet 1905:330). As a trained musician, Mengarini was well equipped to administer the Paraguayan prescription, exploring music's potential as an agent of Catholic conversion in a way his Jesuit colleagues could not. Soon after his arrival at St. Mary's, he taught his new music students several canticles in Salish, two of which he composed himself (Mengarini 1977:101). From there he branched out into instrumental music, forming "a military band consisting of two clarinets, two accordions, three ottoviani and three flutes" (1977:102). He could not have been more pleased with the students he had to work with, stating that the "Indians have excellent eyes and ears for music" (Partoll in Mengarini 1977:200). The eyes, of course, were critical to deciphering the written music Mengarini imported from Europe. In an early annual report to his Father General, Mengarini implored his superior to send a variety of military instruments (including tympanis and trombones) along with new pieces of music with orchestrations. His appeal was in response to his students' interest, which he described as nothing short of "incredible" (1977:102).

Salish enthusiasm for melody was nothing new. For millennia, tribes throughout the Plateau had continually offered melodies in the form of prayers to pierce the veil that separated them from the realm of

"The DeSmet Band." Date unknown.

their ancestors and their spirit guides. Reaching the spirits required a good heart and strong voice resounding with resolve and conviction, an approach that often offended the delicate European sensibilities of the Jesuits in the Rocky Mountain missions. Referring to hymns sung in Latin by the Salish congregation at St. Ignatius Mission in 1894 (established upon the closing of St. Mary's), Fr. Lawrence Palladino, while allowing that "[t]hey sing them to this day not only tolerably well, musically, but with a distinct and clear pronunciation of every word," adds, "Still, we must admit that their congregational singing, particularly when the males join in, has ever been wild and savage-like" (Palladino 1922:99). Bishop James O'Connor found "[t]he congregational singing . . . simply shocking. It sounded as if at least a dozen harmonious wolves were scattered among the congregation" (O'Connor 1888–91:109; Olsen and Connolly 2001:15). These priests were reacting to the indigenization of the hymns—absorbed, reconstructed, and re-sung as expressions of Native identity. By adopting a new hymn and "distorting it in such a manner that it [became] unrecognizable, [singing] it at the top of their voices at least ten times a day" (Mengarini 1977:201), the Salish made the hymns their own, infusing them with the emotion and power necessary to bridge a chasm between worlds. From the beginning, the Catholic hymns were indeed inhabiting their souls, taking a form the priests could not recognize either in sound or in Spirit.

An Indian Hymn Leader Is Born

When Pierre DeSmet arrived in the Columbia Plateau, the Spokan tribe comprised three bands named (by white settlers) for their respective territories along the Spokane River: the Upper, Middle, and Lower Spokan (Wynecoop 1969:7). In September 1880, leaders of the Spokan tribe held a council with General Oliver Otis Howard to discuss the formation of a reservation. The talks culminated in a reservation for the tribe, the boundaries of which encompassed an area traditionally occupied by the Lower Spokan. While Chief Lot and his band of Lower Spokan embraced the new reservation (a simple move "next door"), the Middle and Upper bands balked, reluctant to relinquish indigenous territories for lands that were considered undesirable for their particular needs. It was not a simple matter of geographic preference, however. The Lower Spokan were Presbyterian, and the Upper and Middle were largely Catholic. Owing to pressure from a rapidly expanding populace in the city of Spokane Falls and a growing concern that they might become landless,[2] the Middle and Upper Spokan were forced to put land issues and religious divisions imposed by missionaries aside, surrendering their ancestral territories in an agreement with the U.S. government in March 1887. As a condition of the agreement, they were required to move to the Spokane reservation or another reservation nearby. While members of the Middle band moved onto the Spokane reservation, a majority of the Upper band eventually moved onto the Coeur d'Alene reservation in Idaho, where they could find shelter under a canopy of Catholicism that had taken root decades before (Wynecoop 1969:31–33). They received a warm welcome from the leader of the Coeur d'Alene, Andrew Seltice, whose mother was Spokan.

In the decades leading up to the forced removal from their ancestral homelands, a Spokan family known by the adopted surname of

Indian "Soldier of the Sacred Heart." Date unknown.

"Michael" labored to strike a balance between their traditional lifeways and their Catholic faith. Like many of their Native contemporaries, they saw no conflict between the old traditions and the new religion of the Blackrobes. The Blackrobes did, of course, forcing them to walk in two worlds they would have preferred to walk as one. Kwilshinee, the patriarch of the Michael family, struck that balance, remaining tethered to his traditions while serving as one of the headmen at St. Michael's Mission. He wore a red sash bearing the insignia of the Sacred Heart, acknowledging his status as a "Soldier of the Sacred Heart," a distinguished group of church leaders at the mission charged with setting a proper moral and religious tone (Connolly, pers. comm.; Fortier 2002:29). Located just north of Spokane, the mission included a de facto Indian village, a place from which the Michaels and other

Spokan families could depart to hunt and gather foods in their ancestral homelands. St. Michael's was the first Catholic mission among the Spokan, built in 1866 by Fr. Joseph Cataldo, the first Jesuit to settle in Spokan country. Cataldo arrived at the request of the Upper Spokan leader Baptiste Peone, building St. Michael's Mission in an area that would forever be associated with the leader's name: Peone Prairie (Ruby and Brown 2006:153). The parents of Mitch Michael were married there in 1894, making vows to the Church and to each other that would reach beyond their marriage, to a child whose prayers to a Christian God would be answered.

Mitch was born in 1897 in Indian Canyon,[3] just a few years after the remaining Spokan people had been forced from the city that took first their name and then their home. He drew his first breath where generations of Spokan had before (including his mother, Susan, who still kept a tepee there). In the late nineteenth century, Indian Canyon became a refuge from the harsh hands of progress, sweeping away the region's original people to make room for the brick-and-mortar structures of Spokane. Under this policy of forced removal, Indian Canyon became a final way station that would take families and tribes in separate directions, severing the bonds of generations who had passed and sending them toward a horizon clouded with uncertainty. As Mitch's family navigated this ambiguous terrain between worlds, Mitch became gravely ill. It seemed that the cruel fate that awaited his siblings, all eight of whom died in infancy, would take him too. While his parents prayed over him in Indian and Latin, using all the tools of prayer at their disposal, Mitch made prayers of his own. He asked God to let him live. Years later, when explaining why he and his wife, Mary, were gone so often, he told his children, "I made a promise that I would pray, that I would go to all the wakes there were. I made a promise to it" (Hamill interview with Virginia Matt, July 22, 2009). This promise translated into an unwavering dedication to the God who saved him, built upon a faith that would find expression in the Indian hymns.

Mitch's family had a place in Worley on the Coeur d'Alene reservation, near the mission and boarding schools at De Smet (a town named for the first Jesuit in the Plateau). Mitch was brought up within a Catholic Indian milieu during which many prominent Catholic Indian prayer leaders emerged, including Pascal Moses, Medor Bone, Ignace Stockinghead, Spokane Ignace, Abraham Whee-tsel-ta-ta, Joseph Kwilshinee (Mitch's grandfather), and John Michael (his father).[4] Wildshoe, elected as the head chief of the Upper Spokan in 1890, was foremost among them, transforming his home into a makeshift church where the community could recite prayers and sing Indian hymns.[5] Once a month, Fr. John Post would arrive on horseback from De Smet and hold mass there, standing before an Indian congregation determined to weather the dramatic winds of change with a spiritual fortitude shaped through the generations. For feast days, including Christmas, Easter, and Corpus Christi, a long wagon caravan could be seen trailing south from Worley to the mission at De Smet. The trips to De Smet mirrored journeys made many years earlier by Plateau families to traditional gatherings held by neighboring tribes. They also served to reunite families in Worley with their children, many of whom attended the mission boarding school.

As a boy, Mitch modeled himself after the Indian prayer leaders. He was influenced in particular by Bazil Peone, appointed by Chief Pete Silas (Wildshoe's successor) as head speaker and song leader of the Coeur d'Alene tribe. Mitch often sat with other children in "Baz's Church," an improvised outdoor gathering place where Baz, the self-appointed priest, could deliver his sermons. The kids were spellbound, captivated by the Indian preacher who wore a homemade vestment and knew all of the hymns. Like Louise Siuwhéem, he was an important mediator, serving as a link between Indian tradition and Catholicism that the priests alone were unable to establish. Like any imported priest who became beloved, he was charismatic and engaging, wielding words and song with a commanding voice that ignited the imaginations of his young "congregation." Young Mitch took in every note, finding within the hymns a path to a promise he intended to keep.

Mitch began leading the hymns at a relatively young age, quickly becoming a valued prayer leader among the Coeur d'Alene and other Catholic-leaning tribes in Montana, Idaho, and Washington. His schooling in the Indian hymns came to fruition during a period in which Mitch and his wife, Mary, brought an aging Bazil Peone into their home.

*The Michael family at Minnehaha Park, Easter 1935. Standing in
the back row: Mitch and Mary Michael with their three sons, John,
Mitch Jr., and Sam. Seated in the middle are Spokane Phillips (a family
friend), Ignace Saxon, Jeri Michael, Susan Michael, Arnold Michael,
and Virginia Michael. Seated in front: Lavinia Alexander, her son
Larry, Carl Saxon, and Ramona Key. (Northwest Museum of Arts &
Culture/Eastern Washington Historical Society, Spokane, Washington,
L91-167.53, Richard T. Lewis)*

In a voice still limber and robust, Baz led the hymns for them in long
practice sessions that often carried well into the night. As they sang,
they referred to written translations of all the hymns provided by Baz,
including newer hymns he had translated. During this period, the bonds
of marriage between Mitch and Mary extended into hymn singing.
While Mitch would inherit the role of hymn and prayer leader passed
to him by Baz, Mary was always at his side during the innumerable all-
night wakes they attended over the years, leading hymns and rosaries
right alongside him (Connolly b). Like their teacher, Mitch and Mary
sang the hymns in the same style as those who had come before—
singers who fashioned them into melodies that resembled traditional
indigenous songs handed down through the generations.

Seated left to right: Mitch and Mary's daughter Lavinia (holding her son Larry), Mitch Michael, and Mitch's mom, Susan. Photo taken at Minnehaha Park in Spokane, Easter 1935. (Northwest Museum of Arts & Culture/Eastern Washington Historical Society, Spokane, Washington, L91-167.380, Richard T. Lewis)

The following is a cross section of Indian hymns that were part of this vibrant repertoire during the nineteenth and twentieth centuries. The accompanying analyses reveal a process of indigenization whereby the hymns were transformed, reflecting an indigenous song style formed through centuries of Native prayer and praxis. Although the hymns of the Pend d'Oreille, Salish, Coeur d'Alene, Spokan, and Colville tribes stemmed from the same repertoire, they varied according to regional dialects of a language group commonly referred to as Interior Salish. As such, the following contains dialectical variations of Interior Salish found among the Spokan, Salish, and Kalispel tribes. Words appear as written in *Quáy-Lem U En-Chów-Men: A Collection of Hymns and Prayers in the Flathead-Kalispel-Spokane Indian Languages* (2001). Since its original publication (Connolly 1958), *Quáy-Lem U En-Chów-Men* has gone through two revisions (Connolly and Woodcock 1983; Arlee 2001). Like the 2001 edition, the following text of the hymns utilizes the International Phonetic Alphabet so readers unfamiliar with Interior Salish can gain a better sense of pronunciation. (The impetus for the 1958 edition, an important facet of this story, is explored after the analyses.)

The Indian Hymns

Originally an Italian folk melody, the following was adapted to a European hymn, a notated version of which can be found in *The Catholic Youth's Hymn Book* under the title "Rule of Life" (Christian Brothers 1885). In the first Indian hymnbook produced by St. Ignatius Mission Press (1880), this hymn was set to a question and response format designed to instruct singers in symbolism tied to the devotions of the Sacred Heart of Jesus. It was originally sung by two different single voices, the first representing a person's questions about the symbolism of the Sacred Heart and the second representing Jesus's response (in quotation marks). Each question and response was immediately followed by a chorus (italicized) that sought, in the form of an affective prayer, union with Christ (Connolly, pers. comm.). The Salish gave the hymn its title.

ʔa Spuʔús

(Hymn to the Sacred Heart)

1. ʔa Spuʔús ʔes kʼᵂɫnmáwp.
N'em čn nulxʷ, Yesu Kʷlí?
"ʔaqs cnuɫxʷm. ʔaqɫ nemútn.

Yo ɫu xʷm'qenúlixʷ."
Yo ɫu sx̣ests ɫu Kʷ'l'ncútn.
Yo ɫu st'išs ɫu ʔa Spuʔús.

Yesu Kʷlí, kʷ ʔies č'omístm',

qʷo ntkʷúnt ɫu l'ʔa Spuʔús.

1. Your heart is open.
Shall I enter, Jesus Christ?
"Bring yourself in. It will be your place to sit.

Great is the calmness inside."
Great is the goodness of God.
Great is the sweetness in your heart.

Jesus Christ, I am asking you for a favor,

place me inside your heart.

2. U x̣ʷl' stem' šey' łu sol'šíctn

u es nq'ʷectí l''ʔa Spuʔús?
"ʔanwí kʷ ʔies čułp spuʔúsm,

x̣ʷl' kʷtunt u kʷʔin x̣menč."
Kʷ solší kʷʔin K'ʷl'ncútn,
miʔ solší łu ʔa Spuʔús.
Yesu Kʷlí, kʷ ʔies č'omístm',

qʷo čamúłt łu ʔi Spuʔús.

2. And for what is the fire
   burning
   and filling your heart?
   "For you my heart is burning up
   inside me,
   for greatly I love you."
   You are fire, you are my God,
   fire is your heart.
   Jesus Christ, I am asking you for
   a favor,
   that you burn up all of my heart.

3. U x̣ʷl' steḿ t ʔepł łułuwełcé?
u ʔes łułuʔ łu ʔa Spuʔús?
"T ʔanwí łu t ʔa skʷił t'eyéʔ
qʷo łuʔłtéxʷ łu ʔi Spuʔús."
Kʷ qʷn'qʷéynt, kʷʔin K'ʷl'ncútn.
Mił qʷn'qʷéynt łu ʔa Spuʔús.
Yesu Kʷlí, kʷ ʔies č'omístm',

qʷo łuʔúłt łu ʔi Spuʔús.

3. And why are there thorns
   piercing your heart?
   "It is you that took evil.
   You pierced my heart."
   You are pitiful, my God.
   Very pitiful is your heart.
   Jesus Christ, I am asking you for
   a favor,
   pierce my heart.

4. U x̣ʷl' stem' łu ʔes ʔeyméw's
u ʔes ncaqʷ łu l''ʔa Spuʔús?
"ʔes pimístn łu ʔeyméw's

nxʷlxʷiltís t sqelíxʷ."
X̣ʷl' qʷoyʔé, łu l'es ʔeyméw's
u kʷƛlil', łu Yesu Kʷlí.
Kʷmiʔ kʷent łu ʔan ʔeyméw's
ta qs č'u łu tl' ʔi Spuʔús.

4. And why is there a cross
   stuck in your heart?
   "It is joyful to know that the
   cross
   is the livelihood of the people."
   For me, on the cross
   you died, Jesus Christ.
   Take your cross
   so it will not leave my heart.

5. U x̣ʷl' stem' snxʷul ʔes ʔocqéʔ,

Yesu Kʷlí, tl' ʔa Spuʔús?
"ʔi snxʷul šey' q̓ł malyemistís

t esyáʔ łu t sqelíxʷ."
Kʷ malyém kʷʔin Kʷ'l'ncútn,
ʔin malyém łu ʔa Spuʔús.
Yesu Kʷlí, kʷ ʔies č'omístm',

qʷo malyémłt łu ʔi Spuʔús.

6. U x̣ʷl' stem' kʷtunt sp'aáq',
Yesu Kʷlí, łu l'ʔa Spuʔús?
"Šey' qʷo nxʷuyłtxʷ łu ʔi sp'aáq'
n'em kʷʔi qepł šušuwéł."
L'ʔiqs cxʷlxʷilt miʔ qʷo nc'ek'ʷnt

łu l' spuʔústs łu Yesu Kʷlí.

N'e čʔiqs ʔim'š łu č'nk'ʷuʔ st'ulíxʷ,

n'em kʷʔiqł c'ek'ʷsšn.

7. U x̣ʷl' stem' l'ʔan čelš u ʔes
kʷestxʷ, Yesu Kʷlí, łu ʔa Spuʔús?
"L' ʔanwí łu kʷʔi sxʷsixʷlt,
ʔi Spuʔús łu txʷic'łcn."
ʔi Spuʔús t qʷoyʔé u ʔes kʷestn.
Yesu Kʷlí, łu qs xʷic'łcn.

Yesu Kʷlí, kʷ ʔies č'omístm'

qʷo čš t'iłt łu ʔi Spuʔús.

---

5. And why is there blood
   coming out,
Jesus Christ, from your heart?
"My blood that is going to be
   medicine
for all the people."
You are medicine my God,
my medicine is your heart.
Jesus Christ, I am asking you for
   a favor,
be medicine for my heart.

6. And why is there a big light,
Jesus Christ, in your heart?
"Then you follow my light
and you will have a road."
In my lifetime would you give
   me light
inside from the heart of Jesus
   Christ.
When I move camp to the other
   land,
you will be my light.

7. And why in your hand do you
hold, Jesus Christ, your heart?
"To you, my child,
my heart I give you."
My heart, it is I who holds it.
Jesus Christ, I'm going to give it
   to you.
Jesus Christ, I am asking you as
   a favor
to take care of my heart.

A painting by Fr. Nicholas Point depicting a vision quest in which a Native man is visited by spirit animals sent forth by the Devil.

Another painting by Fr. Point appears to depict animal spirits in a different light. Within the scene, a medicine man (lower right corner) appeals to his animal spirit for help in a hunt. As a result, the hunt is successful.

*In this painting,
Fr. Point depicts
a medicine man
before his spirit
helper. While
playing the flute
the medicine
man is met with
rays of sunlight,
a metaphor
for divine
inspiration that
can be found in
many of Point's
paintings.*

K'ʷl'ncutn qʷo nqʷn'miɫ ɫuʔin tmtmney'   (*God, Pity My Dead One*)

As sung by Johnny Arlee

ʔa Spuʔús   *(Hymn to the Sacred Heart)*

As sung by Mitch and Mary Michael

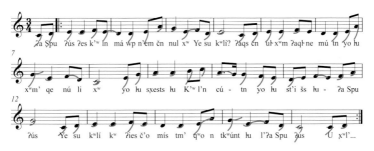

As sung by Johnny Arlee

Qeqs Čšnim   *(We Will Follow Him)*

As sung by Ignace Garry and others

X̣alips Č'awm (Daylight's Prayer)

Kʷʔin Ye su čn es čłx̣al pe neʔ. Kʷʔin Ye su kʷʔin łu-ʔi - Spu ʔus. T ma-
mił čn - qʷ n' qʷeynt, kʷʔa - qs č - š t'im x̣ʷl' ʔin-
š-men' - Ma li kʷʔi Sk'ʷuy. kʷʔa - qs ča - wš tm.

As sung by Joe Woodcock and others

Sl'ax̣t (Friend)

S l'ax̣t tl' čł k'ʷi k'ʷi mu - se? kʷ ʔies we m' qʷo n qʷ n' mint. Č - nes n
xʷc xʷc me l si l'es ʔu lip č n qʷ n' qʷeynt K'ʷ l'n cu tn qeł-mił-x̣ʷ el stis xʷi c'łt q e
tm - tm ney'. K'ʷul'št t šye w's tl'ʔa sp'a á q'. Qs p'aq'- ši tm - lu ʔil' č'im'.

As sung by Joe Woodcock and others

Qeqs npiyelsi (We Are Going to Be Happy)

Qeqs n pi yel si šey' - qeqs n kʷ nem. Qeqs n pi yel si šey' - qeqs n kʷ nem. K'ʷl'
'n cu tn sqʷ seʔs x̣ʷl' sqʷn' qʷeynt łu sqe - lixʷ
t l' n wi st cwa - mist. Cweł k'ʷup x̣est Ye - su. Qeqs

Tempo decreases

As sung by Johnny Arłee

The text of this hymn evokes several images that would have resonated with indigenous Columbia Plateau people encountering the new Christian religion in the mid-nineteenth century. Verse 2 speaks of the power of fire, sacred to Native Plateau people. Not only is Jesus's heart on fire ("For you my heart is burning up inside me") but also Jesus comes to represent fire itself: "You are fire, you are my God." Such an image would have been deeply compelling, an alignment of a precontact sense of the sacred with a new spiritual savior. In verse 5 Jesus states, "My blood . . . is going to be medicine for all the people." The people respond, "You are medicine my God, my medicine is your heart. Jesus Christ, I am asking you for a favor, be medicine for my heart." The reference to medicine as the blood of Jesus, the heart of God, mirrors traditional Salish worldview and praxis, used by traditional healers and valued as an integral part of indigenous lifeways (Olsen and Connolly 2001:15–16).

Like all other hymns recorded within the Catholic Indian corpus, Native song style is evident in recordings of "ʔa Spuʔús." The transcriptions on page 51 were derived from two performances: the first by Mitch and Mary Michael and the second by Johnny Arlee. The Western notational structure represents the original European tune. The curved lines placed over the notation (red in the color plates) demonstrate how the tune was indigenized, a reshaping of the melody to conform to Native song style. Central to this style are upward and descending movements referred to throughout the remainder of this text as *melodic glides*. As is evident in the following, melodic glides can be of various sizes, anywhere from a half step to a major tenth.[6] One need not be able to read music to gain a sense of melodic movements. Simply trace the skeletal upward and downward motion of the pitches (shown in black) while filling in the "connective tissue" of pitches (illustrated in red in the color plates). Rather than prescriptive (written for a future performance), these transcriptions are designed to be descriptive (a musical description of a past performance) (Seeger 1958).[7] Visual markings in red would not be enough to effectively render Columbia Plateau song style, formed through centuries of singing in which the voices of generations were immersed in a unique tradition of Native expression; such a style is impossible to duplicate with distant notational symbols relegated to the printed page (only a flesh-and-blood culture-bearer can do that). Descriptively, however, the transcriptions have much to tell us about a process of indigenization that was extensive, thorough, and complete.

ʔa Spuʔús

Hymn to the Sacred Heart

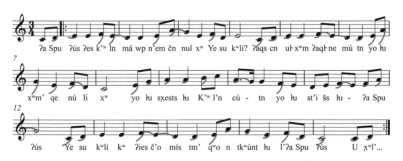

As sung by Mitch and Mary Michael

ʔa Spuʔús

Hymn to the Sacred Heart

As sung by Johnny Arlee

These transcriptions are reproduced in color between pages 50 and 51.

Although these two performances exhibit a significant degree of correlation, there are differences worth noting. In the first three bars of the second recording (including the pickup bar), Arlee makes greater use of upward melodic glides, giving nearly every note additional melodic weight that comes with a longer interval within a sung pitch (the first two melodic glides in the pickup bar cover ranges of a minor seventh). Mitch and Mary Michael, in contrast, emphasize descending melodic glides a bit more, the best examples of which appear in bars 5–6 and 11–12. Such differences are consistent with a more heterogeneous approach to singing style in traditional Columbia Plateau songs, where an individual might employ melodic glides in a manner that suits him or her. Moreover, these transcriptions represent performances by members of two distinct tribes (Coeur d'Alene and Salish), whereas collective interpretations by Native congregations in Idaho and Montana led to different treatments of the hymn. Regardless of such variation, however, these versions of this hymn draw from the same storehouse of stylistic features and, like those that follow, everywhere exude the essence of indigenous Columbia Plateau song style.

Adapted from the Gregorian chant "Dies Irae," very little remains here of the original Latin hymn, composed for the Requiem Mass. Absent the florid melody of its Gregorian antecedent, "K'ʷl'ncutn" is sung much slower to allow for the emotive melodic movements indicative of Columbia Plateau song style. The textual changes are also significant, with a line originally expressing concern for the dead one's sins altered to "what he/she has forgotten," a probable reference to the indigenous Plateau values of paying one's debts and the putting away of the medicine bundle (Connolly, pers. comm.).

Kʼʷlʼncutn qʷo nqʷnʼmiłt łuʔin tmtmneyʼ

(God, Pity My Dead One)

Kʼʷlʼncutn, Kʼʷlʼncutn,	God, God,
qʷo nqʷnʼmiłt łuʔin tmtmneyʼ,	have pity on my dead one,
nexʷ łu snx̣pewʼsts,	also his/her soul,
nexʷłu nłeptmis	also what he/she has forgotten
łu sckʷeys tʼeyeʔ.	which he/she has taken of the bad.

Kʼʷlʼncutn qʷo nqʷnʼmiłt łuʔin tmtmneyʼ

(God, Pity My Dead One)

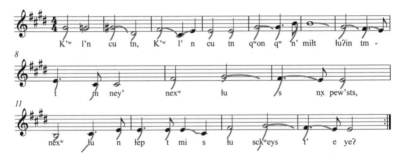

As sung by Johnny Arlee

This transcription is reproduced in color between pages 50 and 51.

In this transcription, Arlee illustrates the emotive power of Native Columbia Plateau song style. Using a blend of upward and downward melodic glides on the first note in measures 2, 3, and 5, Arlee sweeps up to the destination pitch and holds it before casting a downward arch with the power to grab the listener viscerally. In such phrases, one can hear the longing for a loved one recently lost as well as feel the sadness emerging from the shadows of a life now forever bound to memory. In Native song style, one phrase can be imbued with all of this, taking the community into the depths of despair and lifting it up again, working through the pain on the arch of a melody that—like the indomitable spirit of Native people—continually looks forward and moves ahead.

The origin of this hymn is unknown. The only recorded version, sung by Mary Anne Combs, seems to indicate a melody introduced by Jesuits that was quickly reframed in Native melodic terms, so much so that its European origins remain obscured. The words, in contrast, leave little room for ambiguity, clearly reflecting strong threads of an indigenous worldview.

Es cwéɫkʷpi tl' kʷkʷusm

(He Comes Down from a Star)

Es cwéɫkʷpi tl' kʷkʷusm,	He is coming down from the star,
ɫu kʷtunt ilmíxʷm.	the Great Chief.
l' qenplé u es l'cíʔi.	With us he is living.
ɫu ʔoxʷtelt Yesú,	the infant Jesus Christ,
x̣ʷl' stem' u kʷes c'qʷáqʷi?	Why are you weeping?
Unexʷ, unexʷ x̣ʷl' qʷoyʔe!	Truly, truly on account of me!
	(Olsen and Connolly 2001:16)

Fr. Tom Connolly, who has spent fifty years as a priest in the Columbia Plateau, says of this hymn, "I have not heard any hymns speaking of Jesus weeping: 'You're weeping, you're weeping for me.' He's coming down from the star. That's not like any Christmas carols I've ever heard of. So I'm wondering if it's something the people developed" (pers. comm.). Referring to God as the Great Chief is indeed unique and may demonstrate that, for this particular hymn, the process of negotiation between the first Jesuits and Salish-speaking tribes favored the latter.

The Scholastic and the Death Wail

While in his second year at Gonzaga University, Tom Connolly had an epiphany. One evening, while cavorting along the Spokane River with his college buddies, he was struck with the sense that "there must be more to life than this."[8] To the surprise of family and friends, he enrolled in the Jesuit Novitiate in Sheridan, Oregon, the beginning of a fifteen-year trek toward the priesthood. In 1953, he returned to Spokane to study philosophy at Mount St. Michaels, a picturesque but somewhat isolated mission on top of a hill.[9] For many of the nearly 160 scholastics, the objective was to find a way *off* the hill whenever possible, whether by teaching catechism in nearby Hillyard or by running sports in Catholic schools in Spokane. Feeling "neither sufficiently pious nor sufficiently athletic," Connolly looked for another way off the mount. His search led him to Father Dominic Doyle, who needed someone to help him dig a well at his mission on the Spokane reservation. Connolly felt up to the task. From an early age he had built up muscle and a robust work ethic laboring in his father's meat market, stacking, sweeping, and, when old enough, delivering meat six days a week. He made his case and along with a handful of others took a fateful trip to the Spokane reservation with Doyle. They traveled west along the Spokane River, and like the current that seemed to carry him into the priesthood five years earlier, the river brought him further into the heart of his life's work. For the remainder of his two and a half years at Mount St. Michaels, Connolly made weekly trips to Wellpinit on the Spokane reservation, finishing the well and engaging in other projects in and around the reservation. On one such trip, Doyle asked Connolly and others to sing with him at a funeral mass on the Kalispel reservation for Baptiste Big Smoke, chief of the Kalispels, on April 14, 1955. It was the first time he had heard the beautiful and haunting "old Indian hymns" (Connolly a). One hymn, drawn directly from the indigenous song "Qeqs Čšnim," struck Connolly at the funeral that day with visceral power cultivated through the ages.

Formally an emotive lament expressing the pained desperation of losing a loved one in battle, "Qeqs Čšnim" was adapted to serve as a Catholic hymn by Fr. Gregory Mengarini and Salish advisors during the early years of St. Mary's Mission (Palladino 1894:75–76). Sung initially as a death wail for Jesus, it was later developed into a ceremony for Good Friday during which a wake was held for Jesus—another innovation conceived in large measure by Plateau peoples intent on fashioning Catholic ritual and symbols into terms they could recognize and embody.[10]

Johnny Arlee discusses "Qeqs Čšnim" in the context of the Good Friday ceremony at St. Ignatius Mission on the Flathead Reservation: "It was really strong on the Good Friday. Good Friday used to be the big thing. They had big fires all the way around the church. It was a big walkway—went over toward the Ursulines back to the highway and cut across back around to the church. So they had little bonfires all the way around for the procession. They had that figure of Christ that was on the cross, which Father Ravalli had carved. They used to take him down and then they would carry him in a bier" (Hamill interview, August 19, 2010). The procession for Good Friday was preceded by observance of the fourteen Stations of the Cross within the church, during which prayers and hymns were offered at each station in Salish. After singing before the final image depicting a lifeless Jesus being placed into a tomb, the congregation removed the nails from the wooden figure of Jesus and carried him throughout the procession while singing "Qeqs Čšnim," a melody of Native origin with Christian words, sung for those who, like Jesus, had died for the people.

Qeqs Čšnim

(We Will Follow Him)

1. Qeqs čšnim Yesu qe ʔilmixʷm.	1. We are going to follow Jesus, our Chief.
Qs ƛ'll'mi č' ʔes moq'ʷ,	He is going to die on the mountain,
l' ʔes ʔeymew's.	on the cross.
Qeqs xʷic'łt qeqł nxʷlxʷiltn.	He is going to give us our lives.
Qe qes nckʷłls tl' ʔes sulip	He will be pulling us out from the fire
nełi qe kʷentm łu t'eyeʔ u eł ƛ'lil.	because we took the bad and he died.
Nełi qe pulstm t qeʔnple.	Because we killed him by us.
Qe ʔes nmeƛ'm qe sčawawpus	We are mixing our tears
sixʷmłtm snxʷuls łu tl' silips.	with the blood spilled from his wounds.

2. Łu n'e qe ʔes sntk'ʷl'sncutmntm
esyaʔ

łu scnxʷcxʷcmelsts, n'em qe wičtm
łu čnaqs l' šey' u ec'x̣ey łu
scnxʷcxʷcmels. N'em qe c'qʷaqʷ

łu x̣ʷl' t'eyeʔ qe sckʷen.
N'em t šyew's qes pupusenč.
N'em qe nmeƛ'ntm qe sčawawpus
six̣ʷmłtm snxʷuls łu tl' silips.

2. When we are remembering all

of his sufferings, we will see
that another person who alike
has suffered like him. We will
cry
for the bad we have taken.
We will always be sad.
We will mix our tears
with the blood spilled from his
wounds.

3. T łułuwełc'eʔ u łxʷew'łtm łu
spłqeys.

T nƛ'iƛ'imaqs t lp'lp'x̣ʷmintn
čl'čel'šs u sc'uc'ušis
łxʷew'łtm. T smul'mn u
łxʷew'łtm łu Spuʔusts.

T'l't'l'łtm ʔes milk'ʷ u łu sqeltčs,

esyaʔ, t qeyxʷmin u t kʷkʷlatelp.

Tax̣ łu splim'cis u sq'ameltis t
sx̣ʷosm,
u t qʷol'in', u t p'up'unelp.

3. The thorns pierced his head.

By sharpened nails his hands
and his feet
were pierced. By a spear was
pierced his heart.
They had torn all over his
flesh,
all of it, by a whip and thorn
bushes.
Bitter was his mouth and his
throat from foam berries,
and gall, and sagebrush.

The following illustrates the melodic contour of "Qeqs Čšnim," which as in the previous transcriptions consists of melodic glides throughout that build toward a lofty apex, a soaring wail that cascades downward before beginning again. Although this hymn is firmly grounded in Native origins, for the sake of continuity I continue with the format utilized up to this point, laying Native stylistic movements over Western staff notation.

Qeqs Čšnim

(We Will Follow Him)

As sung by Ignace Garry and others

This transcription is reproduced in color between pages 50 and 51.

Once again, Native song style is evident in this transcription. In addition to melodic glides, it contains another feature common in Native song style of the Columbia Plateau region. From a Western musical perspective (sensibilities derived from the Western art music tradition), the hymn employs chromaticism in bars 1, 11–13, and 27–29. These movements fall outside the framework of a standard Western musical "key."

Entering an Ethos of Indigeneity

The funeral of Baptiste Big Smoke was followed by a feast, during which Tom Connolly met Mitch Michael. The solemn event took an unexpected turn as the bench they shared during the feast snapped, sending them both onto the floor. The broken bench perhaps served to break the ice, and the ensuing laughter would mark many events to come during their twenty-year relationship. As they righted themselves and settled back into conversation, Tom asked Mitch about the Indian hymns. Mitch relayed that they were first written down in old books printed at St. Ignatius Mission in Montana. The books had become worn and suffered increasing neglect over the years. While copies of songs were assembled here and there, Mitch expressed concern that young people were no longer learning the hymns. At a later meeting, Mitch asked Tom to help him print a new Indian hymnal (Connolly a). With a reel-to-reel tape recorder on loan from Fr. Doyle, Tom Connolly began (perhaps unwittingly at first) to build on a legacy of religious fusion in the Columbia Plateau that originated with the Blackrobe prophecies of Circling Raven and Shining Shirt.

Recording sessions took place at Mitch and Mary Michael's home in Worley, as well as at Mount St. Michaels, where Connolly transformed the mission basement into a makeshift recording studio. Mitch and Mary sang from their own hymnbooks, which included additional hymns not found in the original St. Ignatius printings. The songs became the stuff that affixed Fr. Connolly to Mitch and Mary, a bond preserved within the reels of magnetic tape that held their recordings. In addition to recording Mitch and Mary, Connolly recorded Indian hymns sung by groups at various Catholic ceremonies and other solo singers, including Joe Woodcock, Mary Anne Combs, and Ignace Garry (the great-grandson of the well-known leader Spokane Garry). The finished product was *Quáy-Lem U En-Chów-Men* (Connolly 1958).

The Indian hymns discussed, recorded in the 1950s and 1990s, mirror the over two dozen other hymns in the recorded collection, all of which are indicative of an infusion of indigenous song style that has remained consistent for 170 years. Reconfigured and re-sung, the hymns

Fr. Tom Connolly recording Indian hymns in 1955. In the foreground from left to right: Catherine Pascal, Mitch Michael, and Mary Michael. Tom Connolly, standing behind the singers, runs the tape machine.

Catherine Pascal.

became new vehicles for spiritual power, propelled by a technology of song refined through the ages. It was effective. In the early days of the first Rocky Mountain mission, a Salish leader anxiously approached a missionary to inform him that "[a]s soon as he would lie down he would hear singing from above similar to that of the animals who serve as guardian spirits to the medicine men" (Mengarini 1977:168). Despite the dictates of missionaries forbidding interaction with their animal spirits, indigenous singers sang Catholic hymns with the knowledge and conviction of their Indian songs, creating new channels for spiritual power.

4

Song and Power

Power, as it is understood in the context of Native ceremonies, might be defined as the energy that first passes from the spirit realm to the individual, which may then be made manifest through explicit methods spelled out in the exchange or implicitly understood within the context of a ceremony or larger cultural matrix. This definition concerns itself with what power is, how it is initially transmitted, and the methods by which it is used. Lee Irwin, in *The Dream Seekers*, defines power as "potency that surpasses ordinary human effort or capacity," focusing on its potential as a transformative agent (1994:69). Combined, the above definitions begin to illuminate in broad strokes the spectrum of spiritual power. As a multifaceted and unquantifiable phenomenon, power is best understood in terms of what it does rather than what it is. Absent a tangible substance called power, we are left to observe how it manifests, how it is used, and how it transforms. At the center of this process often sits the song, serving as a catalyst and conduit by which power's potential is realized.

Power in the Plateau

As the oldest known ceremony in the Columbia Plateau region, medicine dances are central to the spiritual lifeways of indigenous Columbia Plateau people.[1] Though somewhat less prevalent today, they continue to be held throughout the Plateau. They take place in winter (typically in the month of January) and provide a venue for medicine people and others to connect with their spirit guides and exercise their power through dance and song in the presence of the community. On a practical level, it gives those armed with power and song a chance to show members of the community what they can do, whether as new initiates seeking to have their power validated or as established medicine people seeking to retain or elevate their social standing

(Walker 1989:117). In either case, the medicine dance is a forum within which one may strengthen one's control over the power his or her spirit guide has made available. In contrast to the communal nature of the medicine dance, the vision quest is a solitary search for spiritual power during which one pursues a vision, often encapsulated in song.[2] In both contexts, one communal and the other solitary, connecting with power is a matter of connecting with one's spirit guide, the mediator between the spirit realm and the individual. A song from the spirit realm is the tie that binds the individual to his or her spirit guide, acting as a two-way "umbilical cord" for spiritual transmission and discourse.

In Search of a Guide

Vision quest ceremonies of one kind or another have been present historically throughout North America. Though there may be variations in ceremonial practice among different indigenous groups, the goal is the same: to obtain a vision and engage directly with a spirit that may confer power and provide guidance. Discussing the integral position of the spirit guide (*wéyekin*) and its role as an arbiter of power in traditional Niimiipuu culture, Deward Walker states, "The central position in aboriginal Nez Perce religion was occupied by the *wéyekin*, or tutelary spirit, and the notion of power. The *wéyekin* was a spiritual assistant obtained by most aboriginal Nez Perces and was essential for anything other than mediocre performance as an adult. Power, on the other hand, was defined as the supernaturally sanctioned ability conferred by the spirit. In practice, the term *wéyekin* was used to refer to both the power as well as the anthropomorphic spirit granting it" (1985:18). Irwin defines the relationship between the individual and his/ her spirit guide as one of reciprocity and power: "The primary visionary experience is a direct encounter with the dream spirits, who give the dreamer instructions meant to enhance his or her knowledge, ability, and success. . . . Inevitably the gift of power is given as a response to a period of suffering or trial for the visionary. The reciprocity established between the visionary and the dream-spirit is based on the dependence of human beings and the generosity of the powers aroused by human suffering" (1994:139–40).

Though Irwin rightly points out that the dynamic between the visionary and his or her spirit guide is one of reciprocity, it is not a simple matter of "dependence" on the one end and "generosity" on the other. While the individual may benefit from the embodiment of power, the sphere of influence occupied by the spirit granting the power is likewise enhanced, encompassing both the spirit realm and that of the mundane world (together constituting what I have termed the spiritual continuum). The spirit guide and individual become interdependent, engaged in a spiritual discourse that, when activated, allows them to inhabit a shared space that under normal circumstances remains inaccessible to each. While the individual seeks a spirit guide during the quest, the spirit may likewise be seeking an individual worthy of its power. Obtaining such power requires a large measure of preparation. In traditional Niimiipuu culture, older children underwent rigorous spiritual and physical conditioning, enduring the searing heat of the mud and sweat bath and the frigid waters of the Snake River and its tributaries, often back to back and on a daily basis (Walker 1989:18; Ron Pond, pers. comm.). This was designed to build physical and spiritual fortitude, critical to the success of the vision quest. Denied physical sustenance during the quest through fasting, an individual's essence begins to be revealed. Ideally, the ego dissipates, as layers of the manufactured self are stripped away, bringing one closer to the spirit realm (and in the process, closer to death). While suffering is inevitable, the degree to which one can surrender to it often determines success in connecting with a spirit and obtaining power. If one is successful, a relationship is established and power is conferred. Of course, not all relationships of this kind are ideal: "The types of powers granted aboriginally by tutelary spirits were varied, some being quite desirable, others being undesirable enough to require ritual removal. The desirable types tended to cluster around activities such as hunting, fishing, root-digging, warring, gambling, and curing. The abilities granted within each of these categories were diverse and often intricate in application. Undesirable powers were those generally classed as weak, evil, or useless, and great care was exerted during the quest lest an individual obtain such a spirit" (Walker 1985:20). On a certain level, the spirit quest is a courting ritual, as two beings—one physical and the other ethereal—seek to make a connection. An individual viewed as unprepared by a particular spirit may be ignored. Conversely, an individual may choose to ignore the overtures of a spirit.

During the course of fieldwork in the Columbia Plateau, I interviewed Jim Tomeo, who viewed Gibson Eli as both a mentor and father figure. He spent many years with Eli, assisting in various ceremonies while being schooled in the spiritual lifeways of Columbia Plateau people. At one point, one of Eli's "animals" reached out to him. In the following excerpt, Tomeo discusses his reticence to follow in the footsteps of his mentor, someone whom he greatly admired:

> I told him [Eli] about a dream that I had had . . . There was a shaggy thing—I thought it was a big shaggy badger, but the way it approached me—it was crying. It was coming along this real dusty, dirt road that had thick dust on it. And when it walked to me it would go [makes two blowing sounds like gusts of wind], like that. And I told Gib, I said, "I had that dream." I said, "It really . . . at first I was really, really scared." I said, "I was so scared I felt like I wasn't breathing." You know, and then I explained it to him and what it said, and he said, "Well, those things are trying to come to you. You know, that's your decision, you can accept it or you can send it away—or do you want *me* to send it away?" I didn't know what to think about that. I said, "Well, I'll have to think about it at the sweat." And so we did and . . . to me, it's just those things are real demanding, not only of me, but I saw that they were demanding on his family. Things were *really* hard. These things, some of them . . . You had to be able to discern how you would expect them . . . because they would harm if things didn't go right. Maybe when their instructions weren't carried out [they] would harm not only you, but someone in your family. You had to be real *careful* about how you carried those things out. I didn't feel right about . . . I didn't want

to put my family in danger or have them harmed because of
something I didn't do. I told Gibson, "I'm not sure I'm ready
for this, and so I don't think I'll accept, or if I want this for me
here in my life." So he sent it away. And I still don't feel right,
I think, to do those things. A man would have to be single,
you know, without a wife, without children. I have children;
they have children. I *worry* about things like that. And the few
other times I have dreams and things come like that and then
they talk to me and give me instructions, and . . . I pray on it
and say, "Well, I'm not ready. So I'm not going to accept your
offer."[3]

Jim Tomeo has so far been unreceptive to the advances of the animal
spirit. Despite being rebuffed, however, the spirit remains undeterred.
Ostensibly, the spirit believes it has found a suitable person to bond
with, a person with whom to share its power. Tomeo is keenly aware of
the demands that will be made if he were to "accept" the spirit's offer
and fears the potential consequences of not carrying out its instructions
properly. For both spirit and individual, prior experience may be at the
center of this dynamic. Having witnessed the demands placed on Eli
and his family and the risks associated with such demands, Tomeo has
backed away from the animal spirit and its power. In contrast, the spirit
likely continues to pursue him because of his past association with Eli
and close proximity to Eli's medicine power.

Place and proximity are important components here. The spirit realm,
while not bound by physical limitations, contains spheres of influence
shaped over time through interaction and dialogue with culturally distinct
groups of people. The spiritual continuum reflects this relationship and
history. In addition to his concern for family, Tomeo is concerned with
issues of proximity and place: "I find it harder to live like that or to do
that because I'm here in Spokane. I think it would be easier if I lived in
Yakama or Nespelem or Wellpinit—you know—where more people are
doing that . . . I know Gibson said that it would happen anywhere, but I
find it harder because I'm here . . . Maybe I'm not as attuned as he was"

(Hamill interview, February 2, 2008). Tomeo refers to the problem of engaging with spiritual processes beyond the boundaries of a place in which it is culturally sanctioned. Yakama, Nespelem, and Wellpinit are areas on reservations in the Columbia Plateau where ceremonies drawn from ancient indigenous spiritual practice continued throughout the disruptive postcontact era. While it is true that Eli had several very powerful encounters with animal spirits outside the boundaries of the Plateau—a phenomenon explored further in the following chapter—his connection with the spirit realm, consisting of familiar traditions and recognizable forms engendered in the Plateau, was established much earlier in life. Tomeo admits he has "seen a lot of things and experienced a lot of things," but he characterizes his experience as limited, due in large part to not being brought up the same way "Gib was brought up," where the door to the spirit realm was always open.

The Shape of Spirit

Spirits might appear to the individual in many forms: as animals, humans, plants, or virtually any other element found within or beyond the natural world. The spirit described in the above account is atypical, in that its features were not immediately discernible to Eli or Tomeo. In most cases (certainly among those that have been documented), the form taken by the spirit is immediately apparent to the individual. Moreover, the form is often indicative of the quality of power being shared. To embody the power of a spirit effectively the individual often must take on the specific qualities of that spirit, whether human, animal, or elemental. Owl medicine, for instance, embodies qualities of the owl itself. One of its features is the ability to "see in the dark," allowing one to recognize things that often go unseen, such as the darker, hidden aspects of another's personality.

As Theodore Stern has observed, such power conferred by a spirit is often "amoral," independent of social notions of right and wrong (1960:347). Walker likewise states that "supernatural power must be regarded as most often morally neutral" (1989:116). Power can be used to help or to heal. It can also be used to hurt. Historically in the Columbia Plateau, beyond the walls of the culturally sanctioned medicine dance, during which experienced healers and medicine people might engage in something akin to a spiritual competition, spiritual confrontations of a more insidious nature took place. In the process, people lost their health, their power, and frequently their lives. It was a game played outside the boundaries of "right and wrong," with rules dictated by spiritual forces ambivalent to notions of morality.

> One time this *tiwé·t* [Niimiipuu medicine person] was trying to kill another one up the river. He got him awful sick, but he couldn't kill him. He knew it was something in his *ipétes* [sacred bundle], but he didn't know what it was exactly. He went up to see him and asked the sick *tiwé·t* if he could see his *ipétes*. Ha! Ha! The sick one told his wife to go get it, and she brought it out. He began to unroll it, and he took out something and showed it to the other *tiwé·t*. The other *tiwé·t* shook his head, and the sick one kept taking things out. Pretty soon he came to a little flint knife. He held it in his hand and pushed it at the other *tiwé·t* and asked him if that was what he was looking for. That other *tiwé·t* kind of shook his head and said he had to go. He got up and walked out. Before he was home, he was dead. That knife had been enough to kill him. He didn't even come close to touching him with it; just pushed it at him. (Walker 1989:132; bracketed interpolations mine)

Medicine people did not just target one another. Victims might also include nonpractitioners angered by medicine people or innocents associated with the person singled out for attack. In some cases, there might be no apparent link at all:

> There was a woman up in Kamiah [Idaho] one time. A lot of little children began to die. Just all of a sudden they began to die. The people wanted to know who was doing it, and they called in a powerful *tiwé·t*. You know it's got to be one that is

more powerful before it will work. Well they got this one, and he began to work on this child, and pretty soon he had it out. It looked like a little woodworm. It was small and had a white head like they do. He held it there in his hand, and he told the people they were to decide what he should do with it . . . He let them know if he threw it in the fire, that person who had cursed that child would burn up right then. He asked them if that's what they wanted, and they all said aaa! He threw it in the fire then, and that worm began to burn. There was a place in Kamiah where they used to bake qéʔmes [a root staple]. It was just above the mill there. They had been building up the fire to bake qéʔmes, and this woman there just jumped in all of a sudden. She turned around and started running toward the fire. The people yelled to stop her. They didn't know what had happened to her. They tried but they couldn't stop her. She ran right over there and threw herself into those hot rocks and flames. She was just consumed right there in the fire. That must have happened when my father was a little boy [ca. 1875]. He told us about that. (Walker 1989:133–34)

A medicine person utilizing power is beholden not only to laws governing its use but also to its essence. The medicine woman in the foregoing account could not claim complete control over "her" power. Like the laws of cause and effect, her action carried with it a potential reaction—one she was powerless to prevent. While power can be used, it remains independent, channeled through the individual much like the waters of a roaring river: cooperative to a point but not ultimately confined to its banks. Power is rarely, if ever, free, and while power can be used, perhaps even briefly harnessed, in the end it belongs to no one.

Song Transmission

As discussed in the introduction, song, as an embodiment of spiritual power, has been largely overlooked in studies related to indigenous spiritual practice in North America. In "The Importance of Song in the Flathead Vision Quest," Alan Merriam sought to contend with this critical oversight, but while he made an effort to place song in its rightful place within the "total experience" (1965:95), he very quickly walked into a pitfall common in musical studies within the broader context of spiritual experience, embracing an etic (outside) perspective in conflict with Native ways of knowing:

> In looking at the vision quest and attempting to assess the
> actual means whereby the songs are brought into being,
> we apparently have two choices: first, we can assume that
> songs do come to the suppliant in a flash of supernatural, or
> other inspiration, and that the process is therefore practically
> instantaneous. The second and more likely possibility is that the
> weakened condition of the petitioner in the case of the formal
> quest, and the general conditions of expectation of this type of
> meeting with the supernatural in less formal situations, make
> the experience "real" to the individual, but at the same time
> "force" him to be prepared to create songs. In other words,
> the expectation of the culturally conditioned situation makes it
> clear to the individual that he must be a composer of music in
> order to be a successful person in the society. (1965:96)

Very little has changed since 1965, as scholars remain perplexed by a process of song transmission that is counterintuitive to conceptions of music derived from Western musical tradition and at odds with Western ways of knowing. Merriam was skeptical, as many are toward the notion of composition taking place outside of the individual, with spirits as composers. Fortunately, a handful of studies have been more accepting of the relationship between spiritual phenomena and musical composition and performance.

Spirit as Musical Pedagogue

When Native North Americans speak in terms of songs being composed in the spirit realm and given to individuals, they are referring to a phenomenon altogether different from musical composition among humans. Hardly an isolated and idiosyncratic phenomenon limited to Native North America, the phenomenology of song transmission from the spirit realm can be found at the heart of spiritual practices throughout the world. In his work with indigenous Australians from the Daly region of northwest Australia, Allan Marett explores a genre of song and dance known as *wangga*, at the center of which lies a vibrant process of spiritual discourse:

During the late 1980s, Alan Maralung, a *wangga* singer resident at Barunga . . . told me a number of stories about how he had been given songs in a dream. These were the most detailed accounts I recorded of the role spirit agents play in the composition of songs. . . . On one occasion, he described in detail how, on the previous evening, he had received a *wangga* song about a spirit light, which he referred to as a "minmin light," from his two song giving agents, the ghost of a deceased songman called Balanydjirri and a small bird called Bunggridj Bunggridj. Maralung's story narrates how the bird and the ghost came to him and woke him (within his dream) and taught him the song: *"I call the song 'Minmin Light' because Balanydjirri got up and went to it. I was watching him. When that light appeared, he followed it. It was dangerous. He got the song from there. Then he came to me. Bunggridj Bunggridj was there too . . . Next minute, Balanydjirri showed me the corroboree. He gave me this 'Minmin Light' song and I learnt to sing it. 'Boy,' he said, 'are you asleep? I'm coming up. Bunggridj Bunggridj and I are coming.' Both of them came up and Balanydjirri said, 'Get up! Come here! We're going to sing for you.' Then he said to me, 'Boy, you listen. Don't be frightened. Come here.' I said, 'I can see you.' 'Well,' he said, 'we've got to show you this song, "Minmin Light."' I said, 'You come out here and sing to me.' I got that song, yeah. And that Bunggridj Bunggridj, he sang it too . . . Then he [Balanydjirri] went back. 'Don't lose this song.' That's what he said . . . 'Bye-bye,' he said. 'Don't you lose it. You keep this one. I sang this wangga for you.' He spoke kindly like that . . . 'You've got to remember it properly, this good song. This "Minmin Light" of yours.'"* (2005:39–40)

Similar to accounts of song transmission documented in North America, the process of embodying *wangga* songs varies. Often an individual is left to work out the details, to make the song "go straight" after the visionary encounter (Marett 2005:45). Marett discusses this in terms of a collaborative process between the human being and his spirit guides. In this case, the song is not the sole creation of the ancestor or spirit but a joint creation between beings from different worlds. Paul Berliner, in his work with the Shona of Zimbabwe, identified a similar process. In the following, John Kunaka (Maridzambira) shares with Berliner a central facet of *mbira* pedagogy:

> Sometimes when you are learning a song . . . you do not have time to finish it. You may be left knowing only the first section, leaving three parts unfinished. But the ancestral spirits may hear you and offer their help. They can come while you are playing the *mbira* in a dream and tell you to play this key, or that key. Or, the spirit himself can play *mbira* in the dream, showing you what his fingers are doing, so that you can see clearly. He can show you new styles and variations, telling you where to add or to take away different keys. When you wake up the next morning, you can go quickly to your *mbira* and play the way the spirit has shown you. (1978:136)

Among indigenous North Americans, songs from the spirit realm may also be initially unstable. Songs can even be lost altogether, forgotten as the individual emerges from a vision and enters a waking state. This parallels the process of musical pedagogy in which a student of music hears a piece or song and is asked to repeat it or remember it for a future lesson or performance. At first, the comprehension is fragile and may be vulnerable to loss or misinterpretation. The same often holds true in song transmission from the spirit realm, as an individual learns a song. Just as there are numerous distinct pedagogical approaches to teaching music in human societies, spirits employ various methods to transmit songs to individuals, establishing a pedagogical approach suitable to the individual or broader community.

The Waking Encounter

Although I have largely focused on song transmission in the context of the "unconscious" visionary encounter, it has often been found within the parameters of conscious experience. The account below serves as an example of a waking exchange with a spirit, during which a song is imparted: "There was a man who was out hunting. He was sneaking up on the game by sitting at a spot on the game trail when he heard somebody singing. He thought, 'There must be people around.' So he stood there and waited to see who was coming. Pretty soon a spike bull elk came out from the brush and told him, 'This is your song. If you really need this song, sing it.' It was a love song. So he didn't kill the spike, and never killed an elk again" (unidentified Salish individual in Merriam 1965:94).

Encounters of this nature, during which power is conferred while the individual is in a waking state, are historically common in the Columbia Plateau. Although less common today, songs continue to appear in the lucid light of everyday experience. In the following interview conducted jointly by Tom Connolly and myself, one of Mitch and Mary Michael's daughters, Lavinia Alexander, recalls instructions from her grandmother Susan regarding the proper way to receive a song. She then discusses an encounter some years later during which a song was given:

HAMILL: Did your grandmother ever talk about how some of this
    medicine power came to her?

ALEXANDER: About what?

HAMILL: How that bear medicine came to her, or anything like that?

ALEXANDER: No. Once in a while she'd tell about it, but I really didn't know how. But she'd tell stories about a lot of them. Most of the time . . . she told me, she said, "Some of these days you're gonna hear a song. And when you hear that song, you have to talk Indian to it. And then it will talk back to you and answer so that you know what you're supposed to do." But I just [thought,] "No, that's just a bunch of bull, I don't believe in anything like that." You know, I didn't think anything like that was going to happen . . . But then it did really happen to me finally when I was in Chicago—I lived in Chicago about four or five years.

CONNOLLY: Her husband went on relocation.

ALEXANDER: And that's when I was feeling sad. See, Grandma used to always say when you're feeling bad, when you're crying or feeling sad, that's when . . . that's when the animal will come to you, or come and talk to you and tell you not to feel bad or . . . whenever you feel sad or need something . . . they'll send you a song. And that's what Grandma used to always tell me, she said, "Whenever that happens, you have to talk *Indian* to that person that talks to you or . . . if you hear a song then you have to talk Indian." Well, I didn't talk Indian. Even when I was all by myself . . . I still felt ashamed . . . I didn't talk very *good* Indian but I did try and talk Indian at first when I first heard this song. But this song wasn't Grandma's song, it was my own song. I was in Chicago, a hundred thousand miles away from here, from where *I* lived. And mother wrote me a letter. She wrote and told me, she said, "Your dad is sick, he's just sick, sick, sick," she said. "He's pain'in', and he's in bed, and he just keeps kickin' his covers up and he just has his shorts on; he doesn't care if we sees him." And she said, "Oh, Lucy, you should come home, you should come home and help me take care of your dad." And she wrote me such a pitiful letter that day. So that evening I went in the kitchen and I started cooking. I was cooking supper. I was frying some bread and I was crying and I was feeling sad over mother thinking about how bad she must have been feeling

75

and Dad being so sick. And all of the sudden I heard this song. Then I stopped and I turned my stove off and then I listened. "Yeah it is," I thought. "Oh my goodness, it is an Indian song." So then I walked around and I tried to figure out where it was coming from but I just couldn't. I walked and it seemed like it was coming from the window. There was a big window there. I'd go and I'd listen and I'd listen and I went to the radiator. We had a radiator for heat . . . I went over there and I said, "No, it wasn't from there." Then pretty soon I was on the floor trying to find it, but I could hear it; I could hear that. Then I got up and I thought, "Well, Grandma told me if I hear an Indian song I'm supposed to talk Indian." I said, "*Qu'cewét*," but I thought, "No that didn't sound right." And I said, "Who are you?" [*in English*]. I said, "Are you God, coming to me through an Indian song? If you are, all I ask is I want you to go and help my dad. He's sick and my mother's feeling sad and crying." And then I was already crying. And then I talked to God and I asked God to help. And that's when the wind on the window started. I could feel the wind on the window. And then I walked over there and that's when I heard where the song was coming from. And I always say it was the wind song.

CONNOLLY: Well, when you talk about your song you joke about it like it's the "radiator song."

ALEXANDER: Uh-huh, yeah.

CONNOLLY: But you feel in your heart it really was the wind.

ALEXANDER: Yeah, that's what I think.

CONNOLLY: But she jokes about her Indian song, her "radiator song." [*laughter*]

ALEXANDER: That's because it sounded like it was from the radiator!

HAMILL: That's the song you sing to keep warm, huh? [*laughter*]

CONNOLLY: That's the song you sing when you have your [medicine] dance now, isn't it?

ALEXANDER: Uh-huh. But *now* I've already got four of Grandma's songs that's been coming.

CONNOLLY: They're coming? Oh.

ALEXANDER: Yeah, they're coming.

HAMILL: Can I ask, do they come in dreams or while you're awake for the most part?

ALEXANDER: [*emphatically*] No, while I'm *awake*. I already got four of them. See, Grandma has *eight* songs, so . . . I guess they'll all be appearing some of these days, I don't know. I'm getting so old! I'll be eighty-eight! [*laughter*] I'll be ready to push on . . .

CONNOLLY: Well, you have to live a long time until you get all eight songs! [*laughter*]

ALEXANDER: Yeah, *really!*

CONNOLLY: You got to keep going until you get the whole bag! [*laughter*]

ALEXANDER: You know, it's really something. People don't believe in it. They don't believe in medicine dance.

(Hamill and Connolly interview, May 24, 2007)

In addition to focusing on song transmission, the above account highlights vulnerability on the part of the individual as a key factor in the spiritual encounter. It is often stressed in the vision quest that one needs to make himself or herself pitiful, to let go of the ego, the primary barrier between the individual and the spirit realm. The wind song came to Lavinia while her defenses were down. She was vulnerable and, as a result, approachable. Whether a transmission from the spirit realm is unsolicited or within the context of a ceremony designed to facilitate connection, particular states of being appear to be conducive to contact and necessary for such transmission. At the time of the interview, I thought it was rare that songs came to people outside the ceremonial sphere or the "unconscious" visionary experience. For Lavinia it was the rule rather than the exception. When I asked her whether songs from her grandmother came in dreams, she was clearly surprised that I would ask such a question. Her response carried with it a tone that seemed to say, "Of course they come while I'm awake; what's wrong with you!" I found this to be a common facet of song transmission in the Columbia Plateau. Lavinia may have been predisposed to such experience. It is worth noting that Lavinia had a strong connection with her grandmother Susan, one that remained intact in life as well as in death. In the period just before her passing, Susan struggled with an animal spirit unwilling to let go. She was prone to sudden outbursts and was unapproachable to all but Lavinia, who was able to hold her hand and pray for her. Owing to a family dispute, Susan had not spoken to Mitch for over a year, leaving a lingering silence that was making her sick. It played out as an epic battle between spiritual forces with Susan at the center, caught between indigenous and Catholic worlds that threatened to collide.

ALEXANDER: Grandma went to De Smet for First Friday. She got over there and that's when she got sick. Each family had a little cabin there, and Grandma had a little cabin where she used to go, and she'd stay there for the weekend. And she was there and that's when she got sick. Lawrence is the one that used to go see her, and he went over there that one day and found out she was pretty sick and she couldn't hardly speak . . . Father Byrne would pray, pray, pray, and we was all in there prayin' with him and she finally said, "Tell him to *get out* of here." Father Byrne said, "Well, we better go." So they went out in the hallway . . . Father Byrne, he said, "Somebody better notify Mitch and tell Mitch to get down here. His mother's *sick.*" That's when Father Byrne got ahold of Dad. Dad went over there; Dad and Mother went over to De Smet; they went and got her and she was sick and they brought her back. That's when Dad made up with her. Before they left Dad told me, "Get a bed from upstairs and put it down here in the front room, put sheets on it and fix it up 'cause I'm bringing Mother back over here." I was so happy, you know; it made me happy. Dad was makin' up with his mom. They laid her downstairs and Dad just sat by her. But it was just too late 'cause I think she was only there one night or two nights maybe, and then they took her to Sacred Heart [Hospital]. Then she got to Sacred Heart and the devil got the best of her. So many things, you know. That's why I *believe* in the devil. There is a devil— we *seen* Grandma. The devil was in her, even after Dad made up with her. 'Cause he had a little cot outside of her room and Mother'd be sittin' *inside* her room, and Mother just sat there with her rosary and *prayed and prayed and prayed*. Grandma'd look back and every now and then she'd turn and look over to where Mother was sittin' and she'd kind of make a noise, so Mother'd look up at her and then she'd go [*makes a threatening hand and facial gesture*] and do that to her. Mother just closed her eyes and kept *prayin'*. She just kept prayin' and askin' God to help her or help Grandma. Then Dad and Mother used to take turns. They'd go in about thirty minutes at a time. Then Mother would go out and she'd tell Dad, "It's your turn. You need to go back in." Pretty soon he was comin' out. He'd go in there fifteen minutes and he'd come out [and say], "*You* go in there." Mother said he never did ever tell her, you know, that Grandma was doin' the same thing, making faces at him or anything, but she must have been, because the devil was in her I guess . . . So I went in there. As soon as I walked in she turned around and looked at me and she went like *this* to me [*motions for her to come over*]. And I walked over to her and then I went over there and I put my hands on her and held her hand. Then all the time, you know, I was *prayin'*! I was *prayin'* all the time. Then I left, I went out there in the hallway and Mother told me, "Did she do anything *strange* or anything?" And I told her, "No." She said, "What did she do?" And I said, "Oh, she just reached her hand up and I held her hand." "She did *that*?" And I said, "Yeah." "Did she open her mouth or stick her tongue out at you?" And I said, "No." . . . She didn't do that to me. But then Mother . . . I always give Mother the credit. She had a little rockin' chair and she'd sit in there and she'd turn the light down low, and she'd sit in there and she had a little prayer book, I guess that was what she was readin', and she'd sit in there. And *Dad* wouldn't go in there no more. He just stayed out there in the hallway and laid on the cot. Mother was the only one in there with her and she'd sit in there with her *all* night and Grandma would just look at her and snap her eyes—make faces at her . . . Anyhow, Mother was sittin' on a chair readin' her prayer book or whatever she had and she felt somethin' kind of jump across on this side and when she looked, it went *behind* her. And she said whatever it was it looked like a shadow. It was *dark*. So then she knew it was *back here* so she said, "I just sat there and I just prayed and prayed and prayed." That's when she talked and she said, "Who are you? If you're the devil and you think you're so great, that you can conquer everything, well why don't you come stand in front of me? Stand in front of me and tell me what's wrong or what's the matter with you." She said, "'Cause I'm not afraid of you." She said, "Show up in front of me." And just then Grandma turned around and she went like this to Mother [*motions for her to approach the bed*]. And Mother got up and went over there and held her hand and she told Mother, "Pray, pray." So Mother started *prayin'*, prayin' in Indian, and then she went out and told Dad, "You better come in, I think your mother's okay. Whatever it is that's in her must have come out of her. She's okay." So Dad come in there and he started prayin' and singin' the Indian hymns. That's when she died. She died that same night I think. I give Mother the credit. She prayed so much and everything and got help. And that's what I try and tell my kids, you know, it *is* true there is a devil. It's in *all* of us. If you get it flared up, well, then . . .

CONNOLLY: I got the impression when you told me that story before that when she *sang* . . . when your grandma sang, did she have power from a bear?

ALEXANDER: Yes.

CONNOLLY: Okay, so she was makin' like a bear, to bite like a bear.

ALEXANDER: Mm-hmm.

CONNOLLY: So she was kind of calling on her power against their
prayer.

ALEXANDER: Mm-hmm.

(Hamill and Connolly interview, May 24, 2007)

*Susan Michael.
(Northwest Museum
of Arts & Culture/
Eastern Washington
Historical Society,
Spokane, Washington,
L91-167.54, Richard
T. Lewis)*

During her period of illness, Susan apparently found herself
dominated by her animal spirit. Absent the safeguards normally in
place within a ceremonial context, the power of her animal spirit went
unchecked, "flaring up" and becoming difficult to control.

In the same interview, Lavinia recounted Susan's efforts to impart
her songs and medicine power to her. The songs were still coming at
the time of the interview, carrying forth from the spirit realm, where her
mother, Mary, hoped they would remain.

ALEXANDER: See when Grandma was gettin' pretty sick and she *called*
me to the house *again* and she talked to Mother and told

Mother, "I want you to bring Beans [Lavinia's nickname] over
here and put a wing dress on her and moccasins, *shawl, bag,*
everything. Bring her over. I want to see her." Mother *brought*
me and we went over to the junction. Grandma come out and
she had her wing dress on, and she sang. And then she told
me to take all that I had on and she put new ones on me. New
wing dress and everything—shawl, bag, moccasins. Mother had
me all dressed up—Grandma took it and put it in a bundle in
a bandana or somethin' and tied it up. Then she told me, "I'm
takin' this," and she said, "I'm givin' you my *songs.*" And she
had *eight* songs—different *animals.* And she told me, "Do you
think you can carry on and take care of it for me? 'Cause I'm
givin' you my songs." And I never *said* nothin'; I just stood there
and Mother pushed me and she told me to tell her, "Yes, you *will*
take care of it." So I told her, "Yes, I'll take care of it." But see, it
was just before that at the medicine dance, that's when Mother
. . . I don't know what happened and Grandma started bleeding.
So then Uncle Bill, Mother's brother, told me—he was with us
over there—and he said, "Do you know what your grandma's
doing?" And I said, "No." He said, "Your grandma gave you
all her animals she has, so now you have to fight your mother.
Did you know that's what it meant?" And I said, "No, I didn't
know anything." He said, "Well, that's why and then you told
her 'Yes you can, you'll *take* it.'" He said, "Because your mother
already got the best of all of her animals and she's *nothin'.* Your
grandma's dyin'." I said, "Mother's the one who told me to say
yes." But anyhow, that night when we got back to the house
then Mother said, "Where's that *bundle*?" She said, "Bring
it to me." So I brought it in the bedroom, gave it to her. And
then she looked around and she gathered a shawl, a wing dress,
underskirt and everything, moccasins, and a bag. She replaced
what was in that bag Grandma gave me and gave me *this* bag,
and that was Mother's stuff. So Mother gave that to me and said,
"I'm takin' this." Well at the time I didn't really know what was
goin' *on.* I thought, "Well, let her have it."

HAMILL: So your mother took your grandmother's bundle.

CONNOLLY AND ALEXANDER: Yeah.

ALEXANDER: So she took all of that and I thought, "Oh, well."

HAMILL: So did she actually use the songs then?

ALEXANDER: No. Mother passed away . . . Well, Grandma passed away and then Mother started to get sick, then she hardly never did go back to dances. 'Cause I always go with her but she never sings Grandma's songs.

CONNOLLY: She didn't ever sing her grandma's songs—kind of a *hostile* power. Grandma had been usin' that *against* Mary. She probably just neutralized it. I wonder if she *burned* it or just put it away someplace.

ALEXANDER: I don't know. She might've burned it . . .

The "hostile power" to which Connolly refers can readily be applied to the qualities of a bear spirit, which appears to have been one of Susan's primary spirit guides. While Susan was very ill, Lavinia classed the amoral nature of the bear spirit as "evil." It is important to note, however, that animal spirits were (and are) frequently used to bring about positive results. The bear spirit is no exception, being used to eradicate sickness or achieve balance within an individual or group. Alexander and her mother regularly engaged with such spirits in the context of the medicine dance for the benefit of themselves and their family.

At the outset of this chapter, I refer to song as a catalyst and conduit for power, an energy activated and channeled through song. However, to differentiate between power and song runs the risk of creating a false dichotomy at odds with Native ways of knowing. Within the foregoing accounts is an implicit suggestion that spiritual power is woven into the song itself, like strands of DNA wrapped around song's melodic fiber. Can song function as a catalyst, a conduit, *and* power itself? I contend that in specific spiritual contexts, it can. When a spirit imparts a song, it is providing a code for access to power's source. Under the right circumstances, the code and the source become one and the same, fundamentally indistinguishable from one another. At the moment the code is sung, a loop is created within which power, its source, and song circulate simultaneously. In this way, the "conduit" I have attributed to song can be said to reach beyond the song itself, encapsulating all three elements in a spiritual continuum.

5

Gibson Eli
A Case Study of Song and Power

This is given by God to our ancestors because there was no
white man doctor in those days. Now us young generations . . .
if we use it right we still can help other people.

—Gibson Eli

The accounts that follow have been drawn from Tom Connolly's written
recollections and excerpts from interviews—one recorded with Gibson
Eli in 1972 and others recorded by Connolly and myself. Eli's voice and
the voices of those touched by him are privileged here over my own,
which serves only to emphasize, clarify, or elaborate on certain facets
of the accounts for the reader. As "the last medicine man of the Spokan
tribe,"[1] Eli was at the center of a circle of influence that affected many,
including the Michael family and Connolly. The unfettered words of
Eli and those who knew him take us deeper into the dynamics of song
and power in the Columbia Plateau, providing an opportunity to learn
from those whose understanding has been shaped through collective
traditions and corresponding spiritual experiences.

Building a Bridge

Gibson Eli came from a long line of strong traditional healers, including
his great-uncle Steve Moses and his grandmother Ellen Moses. Ellen
was well known for her powerful medicine, particularly effective
against the ravages of smallpox. As a boy, when Eli was struck by an old
pickup truck and nearly killed, Ellen brought him back with traditional
medicines and songs (Connolly c).[2] At an early age, the animal spirits
began reaching out to Eli, seeking to engage him in a dynamic continuum

of spiritual power. His first encounter with his "animals" took place in the hills near Davenport, Washington, where he was digging camas and bitterroot with his mother, Leyton Moses. To cover more ground, she sent him out to dig in another spot some distance away. He quickly lost interest. As dusk approached, he pondered his nearly empty bag. It lay under a ponderosa pine, deflated and distant, ambivalent to the expanding pit in his stomach and the lashing that was sure to come. Eli frantically gathered as much camas as possible, stuffing the bag as best he could. Because bitterroot was less plentiful and more difficult to extract, he dug just enough to place a nice layer of bitterroot at the top of the bag. Sheepish but hopeful, he headed back to camp, counting on the deepening darkness to aid in his deception. His plan was quickly foiled. Infuriated at her discovery, Leyton took a leather strap to Eli and sent him out again. Terrified, crying, and seemingly alone, he searched for bitterroot in what little light the crescent moon offered. Suddenly, he heard a voice, which said, "Look!" At that moment, he was able to see gleaming bitterroot all around him, its hiding places revealed. The source of the voice then came into view: a small, shaggy animal with coarse black fur, unlike any animal Eli had ever seen. "When you become a man, you will sing this song and help people. Learn the song and sing it right for the people." The animal then imparted his song. Soon after, Eli walked down the hill with a bag full of bitterroot and a song he would use to help countless people in the years to come. The spirit (referenced in the previous chapter in an account by Jim Tomeo) would guide Eli throughout his life, often appearing to him at crucial moments when his safety or even his very life hung in the balance. In approaching him at such an early age and during a period of distress, his spirit guide was working to establish trust. In their first encounter, they began building a relationship that would allow one to cross into the world of the other. Each exchange was like an additional girder, placed to strengthen a bridge that would bear the increasing weight of spiritual reciprocity in the years to come.

A Bridge in Both Directions

At the beginning of World War II, Gibson Eli was in his twenties, an ideal age to be called up for the draft. He was anxious to serve, motivated by the loss of one friend in the war and news of another who was missing in action. Although initially declared 4-F by the army (a designation that labeled him physically unfit to serve), he later enlisted in the U.S. Army Air Corps. When he was shipped overseas, his *sumesh* (animal spirit) followed, accompanying him on the long journey to a land far removed from the camas and bitterroot fields of his youth: "Even when there were thousands of men when he was getting off a ship he said his ears would start ringin', just ringin', ringin', ringin', and all of the sudden, in the Indian language, it would give him warning. He'd turn around, 'Who's saying that?' He'd look around . . . no Indians. He would be in the midst of people and they couldn't hear it" (Hamill interview with Jim Tomeo, February 2, 2008).

As a member of the air corps, established in 1926 to provide support for ground forces, Eli was tasked with the unenviable position of hauling supplies through volatile combat areas, manning an unwieldy supply truck under a thin layer of darkness that provided little protection. On one such trip he was forced from his vehicle and took shelter in a foxhole with other troops. The sky was lit up by a storm of German explosives and artillery shells that fell like hail. As he began to accept that death was imminent, his *sumesh* spoke to him in Indian, telling him not to be frightened and assuring him that he would survive and return home unharmed. Some years later, the same animal spirit appeared to Eli after he had a devastating car accident in Montana. He credited his animal with guiding him out of his mangled vehicle and away from death, which hovered like a vulture. As Eli lay in a hospital bed in critical condition, his animal remained vigilant, holding death at bay (Connolly c).

It is safe to infer that the animal spirit mentioned in these accounts, one of many that Eli worked with in his later years, was *very* invested in his well-being. The investment would pay dividends as Eli's power and reputation continued to build in the Columbia Plateau, giving the animal guide frequent opportunities to contribute to the manifestation of spiritual power. In an interview recorded in 1972, Eli discusses the dynamics between himself and his guides, revealing aspects of a spiritual interface through which spiritual power is shared:

MELIOR: You're the last medicine man here [on the Spokane reservation], I think.

SWOBADA: Are you a doctor too, then?

ELI: Well, they call me . . . In a way I don't call myself a medicine man. But many children . . . not only children . . . they come for me sometimes for help. And they got to do just how I do it. I got to go sweat and sleep on it. And afterwards, I work on the people. If they put their faith, put their mind on everything . . . for me to help 'em . . . I'll help 'em. I never did try [it] on a white [person] but I've done on many Indian children—*many, many* on old people. I don't know. I never made it out for myself . . . to do this. When I was small, that's the way most medicine people . . . are abused and taken away. That's where the animals come out to them and talk to them. And when they grow up they follow that. When them things come up to them they follow that . . . That's his own help . . . that's his helper. That's why myself, I don't try to overdo it or something. Before it came, after January, like if . . . you can ask Father Connolly . . . sometimes Father Connolly will tell you. He'll tell you much more. Father Connolly, he witnessed there, he's there every year, at my dance.

MELIOR: You just had your medicine dance, didn't you?

ELI: Every January.

MELIOR: Every January you have yours. Do other Indian people have their dances at another time, then?

ELI: Well, sometimes from first of January or before end of January. It's a mystery sometimes.

SWOBADA: Do you have a special thing that you do during that?

MELIOR: They have to go in the sweat bath, but he has to explain how he does that.

ELI: See, when them *things* come, what I mean by "things come"
... when the animals come, sometimes I'll sweat. Maybe they'll
come in, [with] that song. Each animal's got a different song.
And that's one thing. I can't play with it. I can't come out and
start singing my own song ...

SWOBADA: You couldn't do it now, in other words.

ELI: No.

SWOBADA: You have to do it then when you're in that particular ...
time.

ELI: Yeah, uh-huh ... When them things come it just makes me sick.
Makes me sick. Sometimes I can't eat for a week or something
like that. That's how come my wife, when they notice I'm all
ready they'll have the kids be quiet ... not to turn on the TV
until after everything's over. Like if it comes I can set my date
when to have my dance. I usually have two nights. Some of 'em
had four nights.

SWOBADA: Well then, you *are* a medicine man.

MELIOR: Oh, he is! Is it true, Gib, other people that are sick, you pray
for them ... and dance for them at your medicine dance?

ELI: Yeah.

(Elaine Melior and Henry Swobada interview, 1972)[3]

Eli alludes in the foregoing interview to his process of communicating
with his spirit guides, both before the medicine dance and prior to
healings. Such communication entailed giving up free will. As a medicine
man, he surrendered to his "things" at the appropriate time, doing what
was expected of him. Reciprocity required personal sacrifice. To use
power, to be *used* by power and the spirits that administered it, Eli
had to allow himself to be occupied by them, a mediation of energies
between different entities. The weeks leading up to the medicine dance
amounted to an endurance test for Eli, who awaited instructions on
how to properly set the stage for the manifestation of power. One year,
in early January, he told Connolly

that he never set a date for his dance ahead of time. He had to wait for his animals to come to him. They came first in dreams, where he experienced them vividly. They began to tell him what they wanted him to do to honor them and to help the people. As the animals moved in on him and made their presence more and more felt, he seemed to be in a kind of daze. His mind was filled with what was to be done . . . Each year, when the animal spirits converged on him and he felt their influence was at its highest, he would set his date for the right weekend—Thursday, Friday, and Saturday nights—usually around the third weekend in January. He would begin around 9 p.m. on Thursday night. In the meantime he would go to his sweathouse each night and pray and often spend the day in quiet reflection, eating very little. Rose [his wife] would be busy gathering together the many blankets and gifts that had to be given away and preparing all the food to feed the people. (Connolly c)

Healing

If visions were the main channel by which Eli communicated with his spirit helpers, the sweathouse was his base, a place where the layers between him and his guides were continually thinned to a point where the essence of his own spirit was laid bare. The sweathouse was also a critical component of his healings, opening him up to the vision experience, where the source of an illness and its remedy were often given:

One of Gib's outstanding powers was his gift of discernment— of finding out what was troubling people and where the trouble came from. This knowledge came to him in dreams. Whenever Gib was asked to help anyone, he would arrange first to spend an evening at his sweathouse. He built the fire, heated the rocks to redness and carried them into the small domed, canvas- and rug-covered sweathouse. There he sprinkled water

Gibson Eli

on the rocks to build up a steam-searing sweat and prayed for
the person he would work on the next night with the songs of
his animal spirits . . . After several rounds of cleansing sweat
and prayer and song, Gib came out and cleansed himself in a
cold bath and returned to the house to sleep and dream. In his
dreams his animal spirits came to him and told him exactly
what was troubling the person who had asked for help. Often
it was trouble or grudges in a person's own life or in the family,
sometimes trouble from drinking or a disordered life, and often
it was evil sent against them from an enemy that had secured
the help of an old medicine person from somewhere else. Gib's
animals told him what was wrong, and often he was able to see
who might be sending evil power to cause the harm. When Gib
woke up he usually knew exactly what must be done that night.

The people were told to come that night before 9 p.m. when he
regularly began his work. They would bring their families and
others that might support them in their prayer for help. Gib
would come out in his medicine regalia about 9 p.m., smoke
his pipe, talk to the people about what he was going to do, and
then begin his ceremony in much the same way as his medicine
dance. After his work on the people he would give them
explicit directions about what they should do to straighten
out or strengthen their lives and protect themselves against a
recurrence of trouble. (Connolly c)

Lavinia Alexander (whose acquisition of a song is discussed in
chapter 4) described a healing that Eli performed on her mother, Mary
Michael, who had been sick with cancer for some time. Michael had her
own medicine song, a hummingbird song that, because of her illness,
she had not been able to sing for some time. At the end of the healing
process, Eli asked her to sing it again, helping her to reclaim her power
and regain her strength. Alexander recalls,

He come in there and asked her how she was and she told
him, "I'm just *sick.*" Well, I just left them together and I went
in another room to let them talk. And so they were in there
talkin' and I guess mother told him she was *very, very* sick.
Then she hollered and we went in there and she said, "Get
Gib some coffee and make him something to eat. He's ready to
leave." And so we got him something to eat and then he came
and ate and then he went back, and then he told her, "Well,
I'm going to go. Is there anything you want?" And she said,
"No." Then he got up and said, "Well, I guess I'll be going,"
and went out. Mother told me, "Where's Gib?" I said, "Well,
he left, he's leaving." She said, "Oh, you know I wanted him
to doctor me, but I was scared to ask him." And that's all she
said! We thought that's what he should do—we thought he
should doctor her. So I ran out and he was just backin' out

and I hollered at him and he stopped and I went over to the car and I told him, I said, "Mother wants you to come in and doctor her." And he just looked at me and he said, "Oh, I'm so *happy.*" He said, "I thought maybe she wasn't even going to ask me. That's what I came down here for." He said, "My stuff is all in the car, so I'll get ready and then I'll go in." So he come in and he went in the bedroom and he had his leggings, you know the green leggings he wears and the green top . . . He had it all in the car and he brought it in and then he went in there and he told mother, "Well, I'm going to doctor you." And she was laying on the bed so he went there and then we all went in there and sat on the floor, and that was *mother's dream.* In her dream she seen people sitting *all* around on the floor. Gib told us, "You know her dream that she told about? That you had to sit on the floor?" So we all went in there [*names six people*]. We all sat in there." (Hamill and Connolly interview, May 24, 2007)

Alexander's sister, Virginia Matt, who was there that day, recalls a collective effort to maximize the effect of Gib's healing song:

As soon as he walked in he was all dressed in his outfit that he uses when he dances. As soon as he came in the door he started singin'. Usually when they do that you have to follow him singing when he enters the building . . . So we all started following him, we were singin' and he started walkin' over there. He used these deer hooves on a cane sort of like and he went all the way to the bedroom and started working on my mother. He was talking and she didn't say anything. Then he sang, he danced back and forth in front of her bed. Then he took his hands and put his hands on her stomach . . . Then finally he said, "I got to go outside. I'll be right back." Then he was singin' and he went outside and when he came back he sat with mom and he asked mom, "How long have you been sick?" And she said, "Oh, a long time. I just can't *stand* that pain." He said, "I'm going to go home now. I'm not going to stay because I got to do some things at home to help you." (Hamill interview, July 23, 2009)

In a separate interview, Alexander recounted the dramatic events that would follow.

ALEXANDER: Gib said, "Well, I'll be back in about maybe three days. You should be okay by then. We'll know one way or the other in three days." When he left he was singing. And the next morning it broke. She had cancer in her uterus. [*visibly repulsed*] And that *stuff* came out. And I'm telling you it *stank* like somethin' that I've never, ever smelled before. It's just an *awful* smell. And it just came out and came out and . . . Well, Sis was in there with me trying to help me clean her but it was just comin' out . . . and it's just *green*. And it just had an awful smell. Finally Sis said, "I can't *stand* that smell!" So she went out and then [*names two people*] said, "I'm not going to have anything to do with this!" Well then I helped mother . . . I kept *cleaning* her and *cleaning* her. It must have been at least one bucket full of that stuff . . . I kept cleaning her . . . it took about . . . I don't know how long— maybe three hours or longer. It just kept oozing out, you know, it was slow but it kept coming out. And it finally quit and then I cleaned her up. So after it all came out and I cleaned her up and she laid back down, she said, "Oh, I feel so good." And she went to sleep. So then I went in the other room and I told [*names individual*], "You know, that stuff? It seems like it all must've came out of her . . ." Dr. Hart was there [before] and he said she had cancer in the uterus. But she said she didn't want to go to the hospital, she didn't want to go *anywhere*. He said that she had it real bad. But I don't know, I guess when Gib was there he must have burst it or did *something* and it all came out. I don't know how cancer smells but this had an awful, *awful* odor.

HAMILL: Was the cancer gone after that?

ALEXANDER: Yes . . . Then she started eating. We gave her some soup and some tea. Then on the third day Gib got back over there. And I told him, I said, "Mother seems to be gettin' better" and I told him what happened. He said, "Oh, that's good." He said, "It must be that sickness she had, must've burst." That's when he told me, "You know where her wing dress is at and the stuff she uses when she sings? Put it on her. Dress her up and bring her in the front room." So I went in there and told her we was going to dress her up, that Gib wanted her to go . . . and Gib wanted her to *sing*. So we got her all dressed up . . . We brought her in the front room and sat her on the chair and . . . That was the last time she sang was down there.

CONNOLLY: That must be the time I came out with Gib, right? He brought me out with him.

ALEXANDER: Yeah. Then Gib sang and they doctored her some more. Then he told her to sing and she sang . . .

HAMILL: Did she sing that hummingbird song?

ALEXANDER: Mm-hmm.

CONNOLLY: She got better after that.

ALEXANDER: Yeah. She got better.

(Hamill and Connolly interview, May 24, 2007)

In her interview, Virginia Matt relayed that the initial diagnosis of cancer was made about five days before Eli's healing. A follow-up visit to Dr. Hart by Mary Michael and her daughters left him mystified, as he saw no sign of the cancer he had identified the previous week. Eli made a regular habit of upsetting doctors' prognoses and confounding their expectations, succeeding where many doctors had failed. In the following, Eli gives a sense of the divide between his healing practices and those of modern medicine, incapable of grasping the spiritual dynamics at play:

Gibson Eli in full regalia, Wellpinit Powwow, 1979.

ELI: Once they were going in the night and they seen something like [a] wheelchair. Her husband step on the brake. They stop and come out and search around and there's nothin'—*nobody* out there. [They were] trying to start the car—couldn't start it. Finally another car come and took his wife [Margaret Mason] . . . he's a white guy. This husband, he don't get scared. He's a white guy—he don't know *anything*. But his wife is shakin' and scared, couldn't sleep. When he got back his wife told him, "I want to go." So she called [*names individual*] and [*same individual*] told me. I said, "I'll try." I said, "I can't say I'll heal you but I'll try." I said, "I'm going to sweat tonight and I'll sleep on it." When I did sleep on it, I *seen* it. It was another old lady . . . used her power on other people, to *harm* people . . . That's how come she's in a wheelchair—some other powerful man done it on her.

MELIOR: That's witchcraft . . . isn't it? Would it be like witchcraft?

ELI: Yeah I guess so. He done it on her and that's how come she's in a wheelchair. And she's just jealous, maybe the things what they got. That's how come they turned the harm on her. And here they [medical doctors] just got started in cancer on her stomach. And this . . . doctor, they supposed to operate on her. When they ask me, I said, "I'll sweat tonight and tomorrow night you can come over." When she did come . . . I told her, "You may not believe it." I said, "But this is right. This harm is from another old lady." I said, "Let me give you an idea which old lady: from *your* home." I said, "So now there's somethin' in here. I'll try to get it out." So when I start singin', when my wife start singin', and when I *suck* on that she just screamed . . . in a while she was ready to vomit . . . and she throw up. In a while she [Eli's wife, Rose] said, "Can I take her to the bathroom?" I said, "Go ahead." And the same week, that's when they supposed to get another x-ray of the cancer, they supposed to take it out, cut it out. Well, they come out, they had the x-ray—it was blank. They ask them what they done. She didn't tell them. He said, "Come next week, we'll try again." . . . I told her, I said, "Don't tell them . . . don't tell nothin'." So she still say that I cured her, but myself, I didn't say I cured her. Her husband, in about a week, he asked *my* wife, he said, "I'm going to give a gift to Eli—two hundred dollars . . ." So when I got back from work my wife told me, she said, "You have some call comin' tonight." The call, it was him. He asked and I said, "What's that for?" He said, "I'm so happy." He said, "My wife is really healthy and all that. She's cookin' and everything." I told him no because them things didn't tell me, "Well, you got to be paid." I said, "If she's cured let it be. Give thanks to God."

(Melior and Swobada interview, 1972)

The Currency of Song

The power of the hummingbird medicine Eli used to heal Margaret Mason was encapsulated in the "hummingbird song." It was one of his primary healing songs, utilized in the medicine dance as well as private healings to extract illness from the bodies and spirits of the afflicted. He acquired many medicine songs over the years, including a whale song he obtained from a man on the coast during a stick game (Connolly c). But simple acquisition of a song did not mean Eli was ready to use it. He would have to work with the medicine to control it. While the song was a central part of the equation, many other elements would need to fall into place before he could successfully channel and activate power woven into the song's melodic fiber. The following recounts his acquisition of the whale song and his subsequent efforts to make it his own, reaching out to his Catholic friend, Tom Connolly:

CONNOLLY: But I think what you said reminded me though of the things that come to you, like an old lady at Omack was telling me about it . . . Spirit's like a wild horse; you have to train it and work with it for a long time. And you will ask things of it and it will do them for you and spirit will ask things of you, and you have to do them for it.

JIM TOMEO: Mm-hmm.

CONNOLLY: Gib told you about the time when they were playing the stick game and this old guy from the coast was across from him, taunting him?

TOMEO: Yeah.

CONNOLLY: About the whale song?

TOMEO: Mm-hmm.

CONNOLLY: He [Eli] said, "And my things really got mad at him for doing that and took the song away." But then he said, "You know I don't know anything about coastal [animals]." He says, "You know, I don't have anything." . . . So he asked me if I can get a whale tooth. I talked to this priest . . . from Nome, Alaska. I asked where I can get a whale tooth and he said, "Well, most whales don't have teeth. They have those baleen . . . those fiber things." He mailed it down to me and I gave it to Gib . . . and *then* he [the priest] came out with a real nice beluga whale tooth and sent it down to me. Oh, Gib was *so* happy. He said, "Now I'll have more control over that song."

(Hamill and Connolly interview with Jim Tomeo,
February 2, 2008)

The capacity to control a song, and hence the power associated with it, distinguished powerful medicine people from those less so. The man in the stick game had a tenuous hold on his whale song, allowing one of Eli's animals to simply lift it from him. It is important to note that initially Eli did not want it, as he was unsure whether he could control a song that had emanated so far from the Columbia Plateau. His animal knew better, and by taking the initiative in a Darwinian battle fought within the arena of the stick game, Eli became the clear victor. His ability to eventually use the song stood in direct proportion to his power, characterized by seamless correspondence between him and his *sumesh*. In an interview with one of Eli's relatives, Connolly and I would learn that strangers were not the only ones to lose songs to him. Clara Staneck, a first cousin of Eli, relayed the following:

CONNOLLY: From your grandpa, he [Eli] got two songs that he used, huh?

STANECK: Mm-hmm. Now he's got two of Grandpa's songs. And I never heard his mother's song. I think [a sibling] got it. That's the one he was trying to take away from [same sibling].

HAMILL: How did he take the song away . . . How did he try and do that?

STANECK: With the Indian ways . . . just like he did to me. You [*referring to Connolly*] was with me there someplace where he ran the dance and took me alone. That was his chance to take it away. From there on I told him, "Gib, don't touch me. Don't *touch me*. After what you did, you got what you want. Don't touch me."

CONNOLLY: Oh, he was not trying to help you . . .

STANECK: No!

CONNOLLY: He was trying to take that song.

STANECK: He wasn't helping me when he was going around.

CONNOLLY: Yeah . . . okay.

STANECK: He just . . . *suck* it out of me. I don't *hear it,* Father, it's gone.

CONNOLLY: So he was trying to take those songs from you and your [sibling] that you got from your grandma and grandpa probably, huh. His grandparents?

STANECK: Now he didn't bother with Grandma's . . . Grandma's [spirit guide] is a dog.

(Hamill and Connolly interview, February 2, 2008)

Staneck's revelation came as a surprise to Connolly, who was unaware that Eli would take songs from his own family. Assuming it is true, we cannot know Eli's reasoning. On its face, it appears like an opportunistic power grab. Below the surface, however, it may be a bit more complicated. In the next phase of the interview, Staneck discusses her fear of animal powers:

STANECK: I'd be scared if a dog or a bird would come and talk to me . . . [*laughter*] One day . . . I go to the barn and the owl sits on one of the old trees. It said, "Whoo-hoo." [*Staneck then gives her response in Salish.*] It took three days of me talkin' to that owl: "Are you talkin' to me?" I said, "Owl, talk to me." Boy, did I have the *chills* . . . I ran. Grandpa said, "What's the matter?" I said, "The owl's talkin' to me. He talked *as plain* as an old Indian." From then on, I never talked to an animal . . . Crow will talk to you in Indian. I found that out . . . and owl.

CONNOLLY: Yeah.

STANECK: But I never talked to the robin. I speak to it in Suyapi language [in English]. [*Laughter*]

CONNOLLY: So it can't understand you. [*laughter*] So do you remember what the owl said to you?

STANECK: Oh, I'm scared of owls.

CONNOLLY: You don't remember what he said when he talked to you?

STANECK: He said, [*speaks in Salish*] and then the rest he was saying and I was gone! I was already halfway to the house!

CONNOLLY: [*translates*] "Yeah, I am talking to you." She says, "Are you talkin' to me?" and he said, "Yeah, I'm talking to you!" [*Laughter*]

STANECK: Someone told me they will talk and I wanted to find out for myself. So I did! So even a dog I won't talk to in Indian.

(Hamill and Connolly interview, February 2, 2008)

Staneck's reaction to the owl and her general reticence to engage with animal spirits stands in sharp contrast to Eli's experience, for he invited such interaction. Staneck appeared to have a natural proclivity for medicine power, but she turned away, fearful of exchanges that crossed the edge of the human threshold. Eli may have viewed a song in the hands of Staneck as lost potential, a waste of spiritual power that could be channeled to help and to heal. The profile we have of Eli suggests that a shrewd power grab would have been unlikely. Eli was critical of those who gave in to the darker side of power—medicine people who could not "resist the way Jesus did" (Jim Tomeo in Connolly notes). Eli possessed a moral compass in his dealings with power that appears unique by traditional standards, using power morally (perhaps in a Christian sense) rather than amorally.[4]

Soon after Eli's first heart attack, he had a dream in which a medicine man from Canada took a porcupine quill in his mouth and blew it into Eli's heart. Before it could do too much damage, Eli's spirit guides removed it. At that point, he could have chosen to send the quill back and kill the medicine man. He chose not to, because he "never did anything like that" (Connolly c). Morality is often in the eye of the beholder, and we cannot know for sure where Eli drew the line. One thing is certain: given the right circumstances, he would take a song—whether from someone who had tried to demean him in the stick game or from someone much closer to home. We also know he made full use of songs in his possession. He knew the rules governing their use and where he stood within the framework of spiritual power, not as one who harms but as one who heals, an ideal reinforced—in all likelihood—by his personal encounter with Catholicism.

6

Medicine and Miracles

In 1969, Mitch Michael approached Fr. Connolly with news that Gibson Eli wanted to become a Catholic. Although Eli had never attended church as a boy, his relatives on the Moses side (belonging to the band of Upper Spokan) were largely Catholic, as was his wife, Rose. In August of that year, at the age of fifty-six, he was baptized by Connolly at his home in Hillyard, just north of Spokane. Mitch and Mary Michael stood at his side during the baptism in their new role as godparents, making a commitment to Gib that extended beyond friendship into a spiritual realm that, in addition to accommodating the power of the animal spirits, now included the power of the Holy Spirit. The baptism also marked the beginning of a spiritual odyssey for Connolly, who would soon experience a spiritual conversion of his own.

Like many of his Native contemporaries, Eli saw no conflict between Catholicism and his Native traditions (God apparently did not either, as demand for Eli's services as a medicine man and healer only increased after his baptism). By standards set by the first Jesuits in the Columbia Plateau, he would have been labeled a sinner, engaging in decidedly un-Catholic ceremonies and communicating with unsavory spirits. Worst of all, he continued to participate in one of the more unseemly Indian pastimes, the stick game.[1] To the Blackrobes, the stick game was a perverse display of loutish gambling. Allowed a more comprehensive view, they would have been even more horrified to learn that just below the surface of the stick game the animal spirits were at play. Within the context of this "game," participants engaged in a spiritual wrestling match of sorts, in which power-infused songs, some of them ancient, separated the winners from the losers. During Eli's time, it was not just money or goods that were lost during the stick game, but songs themselves as one singer overpowered another. Unlike his Jesuit predecessors, Connolly grasped the spiritual dynamics hidden from view:

In the stick games, Gib and Rose sat side by side throughout the night, betting, singing, hiding, and guessing the bones. The songs they sang were ancient chants, forms of power songs given by the animal spirits in dreams to ancestors long ago. While hiding the bones on their side of the game, they sang power songs that came down through their families, calling on the power of the animals to prevent the guesser on the other side from "seeing" in which hand they were hiding the plain white bone. . . . They also had great psychic gifts to read minds and tell which hand held the unmarked bone. But most of the old-timers knew how to call their animal guardian spirits through song and gesture to help them win over the players on the other side. The animal spirits gave power to win in stick games, and sometimes these animals also had powers that could be used to help people in other ways. Over the years, as Gib and Rose became stronger at stick games, they sat down to collect the money and run their own games. Then it became serious, and often people with power on the other side would call upon their animals to defeat Gib. Sometimes they might challenge Gib in song and gesture, as though they had power and he had none. But as his power grew stronger over the years, Rose might tell him: "you can take that song away from him." Gradually the challenger might falter and lose to Gib. His song had lost its power, and on several occasions that song and the power of the animal actually left the challenger and was captured by Gib's own animals. He might use the song later to defeat other stick game challengers or perhaps to help people in his healing ceremonies. Sometimes people with lesser power would get hurt or bothered after challenging those with greater power in the stick game. Gib said that sometimes he couldn't help it. His animal spirits didn't like being made fun of by a challenger, and they sometimes seemed to reach out on their own to capture an opponent's song or bother him in some way.[2]

Gibson Eli and his wife Rose at a stick game in Soap Lake, Washington, 1967. At the center stands Madeline Moses with bones in hand. Gibson is seated to her left, playing the drum and singing. Rose is kneeling directly to her right. Their daughter Libby, also singing, is seated directly behind Gibson's right shoulder.

Growing increasingly comfortable in this context, Connolly found himself in territory forbidden by his Jesuit predecessors, directly engaging in the dynamic of spiritual power in the stick game:

Once, I heard him singing his stick game song at the Wellpinit powwow. I went over to stand behind him. He was singing and hiding bones, playing against a team run by an old couple from the Colville reservation. The man was trying to "guess" Gib. I tried to support Gib by concentrating as much energy as possible and sending it against the old man to prevent him from seeing in what hand Gib was holding the plain white bone. The old man tried to read Gib for a long time, finally shaking his head he passed his set of bones to his wife to try to "match"

Gib. She held the bones, I switched my energy against her, and all of a sudden she looked right up at me. I was embarrassed, because I felt that a priest shouldn't be taking sides in these kinds of traditional contests—kind of like a kid caught with his hand in the cookie jar! So I reacted by looking down neutrally and dropping my concentration. After that she matched Gib's bones and won that round. (Connolly c)

During the stick game, Eli strengthened the bonds between himself and his spirit guides and the power they granted. But power had a price. The songs given to Eli came with instructions regarding their use and what was expected in return. His relationship with his spirit helpers was reciprocal, and each guide had specific requests. Some might require that particular foods be given away in their honor. Others might specify certain gifts. Eli had to honor them all evenhandedly, and with each new song came more responsibility (Connolly c).

As a conduit for increasing spiritual power, Eli was often stretched very thin. On occasion, overwhelmed and dizzy from the demands of his animals, he would seek solace in the numbing effects of alcohol. When he was drinking, the spirits were unable to reach him, providing Eli a respite from their influence, which was often incessant (Hamill and Connolly interview with Jim Tomeo, February 2, 2008). During one such episode, Rose shared with Connolly that Eli was at a bar somewhere in downtown Spokane. Connolly asked around and found him at the Buck and Doe, a popular spot where Native people in the area went to both forget and remember. It was a gathering place where the persistent pain of being Indian could be lost in the clamor of communal connections temporarily rekindled. Afraid to go home for fear of what Rose might do, Eli was relieved when Connolly offered to run interference, promising to stay the night so he might be spared the fallout from Rose's mounting anger. It was a meaningful gesture to Eli, inspiring him to quit drinking and to find other ways to manage his animal spirits.

Out of gratitude, he began to share details about his medicine dance with Connolly (Connolly, pers. comm.). As a valued healer, Eli hosted his own medicine dance every January, where family and friends, including many he had healed, gathered to participate in spiritual power made manifest. In January 1970 he went even further, inviting Connolly to his dance. Connolly's presence caused some alarm, as a priest had never before attended a medicine dance in the Columbia Plateau. Connolly shares his experience:

> When I came in the dimly lit hall, Rose motioned me over to sit
> next to Gib. He was sitting on several Pendletons [blankets] on
> the floor and quietly smoking his pipe. It was just 9 p.m., and
> he was waiting for me to arrive. Gib kept a small stone pipe
> and wooden stem wrapped in calico cloth with his mixture of
> tobacco and native dried kinnikinnick leaves, and he smoked
> quietly and prayerfully, thinking of his animals and what was
> to be done. . . . When Gib felt that everything was ready, he
> started to sing his first song in the center of the hall. Rose
> picked up the song with him, and everyone in the room joined
> in. It was the song of the wolf, similar to the wolf power that
> his grandmother had used to save his life when he had been run
> over so many years before . . . The song soared . . . and after a
> number of rounds of the open vowel singing, he began to give
> directions to the people during the singing. The song itself had
> no words, but Gib spoke his own words softly to his second—a
> helper who stood at his side in the middle of the room. The
> second shouted out the words to the people, phrase by phrase,
> in Indian, while everyone else continued the singing of the song.
> After 15 minutes or so, the directions had been completed, and
> the energy of the song had caught and focused the energies of
> everyone in the room, and had begun the calling of the animal
> spirits to be present throughout the night.[3] After the opening
> song of the wolf . . . Gib started singing the song of another
> animal that he used to prepare and protect the hall and the
> people during the ceremonies. Everyone joined him in this new
> song, as Gib looked around the hall and over the people. He
> was sensing what needed to be done to cleanse the hall from

any wrong energies—things that might have happened here before or any ill feelings that people might have brought in with them. Then he moved throughout the room, praying for the people and for the cleansing of the hall itself . . . After another song or so, Gib explained to the people through his second why he had invited me there for his dance. He explained that we had been working together, that Mitch and Mary had brought me to his home to baptize him and that when he was downtown in trouble with Rose that I had come to find him and return back home with him. It was in gratitude for this that he had invited me to come. Then through his second he called me to the floor and gave me a dark blue Pendleton blanket in appreciation of our friendship. Many people had been surprised to see a priest at the dance, since the Church had always condemned these medicine dances for so many years. One woman who knew that I'd be there told her children not to look at me when they came into the hall. I could be bringing new kinds of spiritual energies into the hall, and people didn't know what it might do. But Gib explained that this was the way he wanted things and they shouldn't be worried about anything. (Connolly c)

During the medicine dance Eli had other things to worry about, concerns rooted in age-old spiritual dynamics at play in the Columbia Plateau:

Later in the ceremony a bucket of water was brought in so people could have a drink. Gib sang over the water to ensure that it would be helpful and not harmful. Then he would drink from the ladle and his helpers would pass the water around for all to drink. At a given time, Gib would also announce a bathroom break, with a protective song, while the women went outside on one end of the hall, and the men went out on the other end. Because there were so many spirits that could help or hurt, and so many people with power that might be jealous of Gib or with bad intentions towards those who came to the dance, it was always important to protect the hall from any uninvited presence. It had to be kept as a sacred space in which his good spirits could do good things for people, without any interference. (Connolly c)

That night, Fr. Connolly was brought into the fold of a dynamic spiritual continuum that few outside of the Native community had experienced. He walked through a door his predecessors had struggled to keep shut and sat next to a friend with whom he shared a hunger for the sacred. Together they would cross lines laid by religious men in an effort to reach across the boundaries of faith and touch the universal divine. As they grew closer, Eli asked Connolly to accompany him to various healings outside of Spokane. During these sessions, Connolly often sang Eli's healing song while Eli worked on people. Connolly witnessed inexplicable and miraculous healings during this time, the likes of which he had only read about in the Bible. His experiences with Gib contributed to an acceptance of a precontact spiritual worldview, one at odds with the religious worldview held by Jesuits who preceded him:

Despite the fact that earlier generations of priests had not understood the good use of medicine power and had preached

Gibson Eli and Fr. Tom Connolly on the Colville Reservation, 1977.

strongly against it, I felt comfortable working with Gib. I saw
the results of his work in helping people, and I knew that he
recognized the power of his animals as coming from God rather
than from any other source. I felt that Gib used his powers very
much according to the teachings of Jesus—that all power came
from God rather than from ourselves and that credit went to
Him rather than ourselves. Gib never bragged about what he
could do, and the rest of the time he said that he would help if
he could. He never demanded or would accept payment of any
kind from people, while other medicine men might often charge
their patients a great deal in money or blankets. Most of all,
Gib was very strong on forgiveness and not holding anything
against anyone else. Often it seemed, in the Indian way, that
evil power or energy had been sent against people to hurt them
by their enemies who had gone to other medicine people to
send the evil. It was sometimes common for a medicine man to
take this evil power out of the afflicted one and send it back to
attack whoever had originally sent it.[4] But Gib would never
do this. He told people he would try to take the evil away from
them and get rid of it. But he would never use power to hurt
anyone else. (Connolly c)

Referring to a process of personal transformation that took place
during Eli's healings, Connolly reflects on spiritual "realities" that led
him to equate the animal spirits with angels:

To me they're angel spirits. When Gib was working on people
I'd try and visualize—in a prayerful kind of meditative way—
like when he was singing his mother wolf song, calling all
the children out of the forest, or calling on the hummingbird
helper when he was trying to draw the evil out of people he
was working on. In my way I would see them as angelic spirit
helpers from God. I was trying to be as much a part of that
as I could and energize that reality . . . I was aware of calling

down power from God, through Jesus and the spirits of nature and the animals, through Gib and the work that he was doing for people. I sometimes visualized bright rays of energy coming down directly into him, and sometimes through his specific animal spirit to him. (Hamill interview, February 2, 2008)

The Indian Wake

Connolly's personal transformation—a process by which he would embrace a new religious worldview—was gradual. Years before he met Gibson Eli, Connolly began operating within an ethos of indigeneity. From the moment he heard "Qeqs Čšnim" at the funeral of Baptiste Big Smoke (the "first day of the rest of his life"), he became increasingly immersed in Native ways of knowing. From the start, Mitch Michael was his teacher, schooling him in aspects of Catholic Indian rituals rooted in Native epistemologies a world away from his studies at the Jesuit Novitiate. Through Michael, Connolly was exposed to a uniquely indigenized form of Catholic expression, the Indian wake. Next to the hymns themselves, the Indian wake represented a critical mediation wrought during the early days of the Rocky Mountain missions. At the helm were prayer leaders like Michael, as essential as an undertaker or priest when it came to seeing people into the afterlife. The following is a composite of the many wakes Michael and Connolly conducted together, highlighting an ethos of indigeneity that led to a significant transformation of the Catholic mass.

In "Wakes, Funerals, and Feast Days," Johnny Arlee discusses the function of the Indian wake, reflecting Native values rooted in community: "The healing of hurt caused by death in the way of our ancestors is good. All the acts performed at a wake or gathering are acts of prayer and sacrifice. Each is as important as the next. Cooking, washing dishes, sweeping floors, serving coffee or a drink of water, sending flowers, offering a prayer at home, leading songs and prayers, running errands, sending food, filling in the grave, being a pallbearer, babysitting—each contributes to the whole" (n.d.:1). In

111

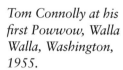

Tom Connolly at his first Powwow, Walla Walla, Washington, 1955.

addition to taking care of the needs of the deceased and the grieving, wakes conducted by tribes in the interior Northwest place a particular emphasis on collective healing and communal integrity, viewing the process—from the wake to the memorial giveaway—as an opportunity to heal old wounds and strengthen communal bonds. Prayer leaders, beyond offering important prayers and hymns, are tasked with setting a tone conducive to collective cohesion, visiting with the family of the deceased to temper the anguish associated with death while guiding them and others toward unified expressions of prayer.

When Bazil Peone (Mitch Michael's primary teacher) was an active prayer leader, wakes were held for three days in the family residence of the deceased. Homes were transformed before such occasions, with furniture removed to make room for members of the community, who might sit on chairs, on benches, or directly on the floor. If many people were in attendance, the feast might be moved outdoors to a makeshift

Fr. Tom Connolly in full regalia.

kitchen made of canvas and tepee poles.[5] The three-day wake was an important innovation necessitated by a spiritual phenomenon common in the Columbia Plateau prior to contact.[6] Johnny Arlee discusses this age-old tradition, one in which people often returned from the land of the dead with teachings and songs for the benefit of the People:

> Stories from our elders tell us that the dead were wrapped in white buckskins or blankets and buried. When time came of the Blackrobes, cemeteries were introduced. When bodies were dug up for transferring to the cemeteries, some of them were found to have changed positions and were not actually dead but in a deep sleep. From that time the priests suggested having three-day wake services in case the dead person came back to life. This is very similar to Christ's time when He died; He laid in the tomb three days and was risen. In the early 1900's, a man

known as Sam Resurrection came back to life during his own wake service. After that for the remaining part of his life he would attend wakes, whether he knew the deceased or not. He would walk many miles to attend a wake, leading in prayer and sharing comforting words for the bereaved family. (n.d.:2)

Although the practice of the three-day wake was initiated and endorsed by priests (we do not know by whom), it is unlikely that they were making room for a process in which an individual might come "back to life." Rather, they would have viewed such a phenomenon as an aberration in which members of their Native congregation occasionally fell into a "deep sleep" (so deep, in fact, that there was no perceptible breath or heartbeat). The priests had little choice. Paramount to their faith was the belief that there was but one resurrection, reserved for Jesus alone. Oral histories throughout Native North America suggest otherwise, pointing to a process by which individuals passed through the threshold of physical death and returned.[7] In the Columbia Plateau, the story of Jesus's own resurrection would have been particularly meaningful, another point of resonance for indigenous Plateau peoples encountering a foreign religion.

During his time as a prayer leader, Mitch Michael was called to wakes, which might be held for anywhere from one to three days. Increasingly, they took place at community centers or tribal longhouses, both of which were becoming more common in tribal communities and were well equipped to accommodate large groups of people. Whether at home, in a community hall, or in a longhouse, the undertaker would arrive in the afternoon. As prayer leader, Michael would be there to greet him, helping him carry the casket indoors, where it could be placed for viewing. The first to come upon the deceased were the immediate family. As they approached, Michael, along with his wife, Mary, often recited a rosary prayer to soften the visceral pangs of loss that accompanied death. The prayer would be followed by an Indian hymn, the first opportunity for those in attendance to cut a path for their friend and loved one into the afterlife, each voice a melodic sickle wielded through song. Like the songs that preceded the Blackrobes, the hymns were formed of the familiar sounds of Salish, guiding the soul back to its source in a primordial language spoken from the Beginning. After additional hymns and prayers, Michael would often stand and offer some final words of solace before others were invited to approach the body, beginning the process of letting go and saying goodbye.

Before dinner, Michael would offer prayers in Salish, echoing indigenous values of honoring the foods that fed the living. Fr. Connolly would arrive shortly thereafter, visiting with family and friends before offering a rosary. With Connolly's arrival, leadership during the wake became a joint effort. Michael and Connolly stood at two ends of a spectrum, the center of which was as Native as it was Catholic. This middle ground was formed early on in the Rocky Mountain missions,

Mitch and Mary Michael with two of the Blackrobes. Fr. Paul Sauer stands to the right of Mary, Fr. Cornelius Byrne stands to the right of Mitch. The tepee in the background, made by Mary Michael, was big enough to conceal a car, a surprise gift for Fr. Byrne. (Northwest Museum of Arts & Culture/Eastern Washington Historical Society, Spokane, Washington, L91-166.128, Richard T. Lewis)

but unlike the Jesuits who had preceded him, Connolly listened, taking in the indigenousness of the wake with open ears and an open heart. He looked to Mitch for guidance, inspired by Mitch's dedication to the job. After the rosary, the floor was open for anyone to offer words on behalf of the deceased and for the benefit of those he or she left behind (Arlee n.d.:3), words reflecting Native values of honoring the dead (Connolly b). Expressions of sentiment and song would continue, interrupted only by the midnight meal—foods accompanied by a prayer to nourish the body and spirit.

Johnny Arlee discusses the night that would follow, stressing the importance of resisting the overtures of sleep while remaining vigilant and focused: "We try our best to protect these special sacrifices which are left for the loved one. The hardest times are from midnight to daybreak. It is said by the elders that it is at night when the evil spirits move about. We must stay awake at that time to protect the prayers and offerings which are left for the loved one and the family. If we should all fall asleep, we don't know where the prayers or offerings will end up" (Arlee n.d.:3).

After a night of guarding the offerings and prayers, Michael, along with those in attendance, would greet morning's first light with the Indian hymn "X̱alips Č'awm" (Daylight's Prayer) (Olsen and Connolly 2001:16). All-night ceremonies and morning songs were common among Columbia Plateau tribes before contact, and the use of "X̱alips Č'awm" in the context of all-night wakes represents another important mediation between indigenous peoples and Jesuits. In the mid-1840s Fr. Mengarini discussed a "night-long vigil during which [the Salish] alternate the recitation of prayers, especially the rosary, with the singing of hymns as they circle the corpse," referring to Salish traditions brought into a reconfigured and indigenized Catholic wake (Mengarini 1977:168). The words to "X̱alips Č'awm" describe meeting the daylight with Jesus:

X̣alips Č'awm

(Daylight's Prayer)

Kʷʔin Yesu, čnes čłx̣alpeneʔ.	You my Jesus, I am meeting the daylight.
Kʷʔin Yesu, kʷʔin łuʔi Spuʔus.	You my Jesus, you are my heart.
Tma mił čn qʷn'qʷeynt,	Because I am very pitiful,
kʷʔaqs čšt'im x̣ʷl' ʔin šmen'.	you are going to protect me from my enemy.
Mali kʷʔi Sk'ʷuy.	Mary, you are my mother,
kʷʔaqs č'awštm.	you are going to pray for me.

X̣alips Č'awm

(Daylight's Prayer)

As sung by Joe Woodcock and others

This transcription is reproduced in color between pages 50 and 51.

The term *pitiful*, found in many hymns, reflects the Native value of humility. While acknowledging human weakness and folly, it holds within it the promise of personal growth and redemption. The state of being pitiful, of acknowledging one's place in a world consisting of powers beyond human control, meant that Native peoples in the Columbia Plateau were particularly primed to bring the prophet Jesus and an all-powerful God into an extant worldview, shaped by Native prophets who had come before.

Once again, we see in this transcription the melodic glides discussed in chapter 3, indicative of Native Columbia Plateau singing style. Like "Qeqs Čšnim" (We Will Follow Him), "X̱alips Č'awm" comes from a song of Native origin. It largely moves within a pentatonic framework common to traditional Native songs of the Columbia Plateau. At bar 12, however, there is a shift. The introduction of the D on the second beat of that measure temporarily pulls the hymn out of a Native feel and structure. It behaves like a European cadence, hinting, just for a moment, at something akin to D major. The same happens in the final bar. This may indicate that the hymns being sung in the early Rocky Mountain missions—a majority of which were built on European tunes—led to the inclusion of a standard European cadence within the framework of a Native song. This suggests that while Native Catholics were indigenizing the hymns, they were also adopting foreign musical structures and sensibilities, in the process making them their own. Another possibility is that Mengarini added the cadence to bring "X̱alips Č'awm" into compliance with the repertoire of hymns being developed at the mission. Either way, a significant musical transformation occurred, one that has remained intact for 150 years.

After the morning hymn, breakfast was served, followed by additional prayers and Indian hymns. With the family seated in the front row, Michael would announce the final opportunity to approach the body of the deceased—all that remained in this world of the person whose spirit now made its way to the next. While friends and loved ones filed around the casket, Mitch and Mary would offer the hymn for departed souls: "Sl'ax̱t" (Friend). In this hymn, a desperate soul is imprisoned within the "small fire" that is purgatory, calling out to a friend in search of redemption and release. After Jesus, Mary, and God "turn their faces" away, the individual beseeches the Blackrobe to help repay his or her considerable debt by "offer[ing] up the blood of Jesus Christ to God." Rather than viewing purgatory as a way station after death for imperfect souls still troubled by sin, Johnny Arlee equates it to earth, casting the voice of the individual in the following as one of many terrestrial voices seeking a path to God. Those in the chorus, rather than singing from the earth, sing from heaven, asking God to shine a light into the darkness that imprisons us all. Arlee's interpretation is significant, reflecting a Native worldview in which sufferings and sin are not carried over into the afterlife but are shed, as one is freed from the confines of one's body and the gravity of earth.

Sl'aχt

(Friend)

1. Sl'aχt, tl' čłkʷ'ikʷ'imuseʔ	1. Friend, from the small fire [purgatory]
kʷʔies wem', qʷo nqʷn'mint.	I am calling you, have pity on me.
Čnes nxʷcxʷcmelsi	I am suffering
l'es ʔulip, čn qʷn'qʷeynt.	in the fire, I am pitiful.
Chorus: K'lʷncutn, qeł miłχʷelstis	*God, it's going to be his rest/ peace*
xʷic'łt qe tmtmney'.	*given to our dead one.*
K'ʷul'št t šyew's tl' ʔa sp'aáq'.	*Make for him always your light.*
Qs p'aq'šitm lu ʔi l' č'im'.	*It will give him light there in the darkness.*
2. Ye solši tast'ul' swilwlt.	2. This fire is very powerful.
Nχal'utm łu ʔi l' č'im'.	It is frightening in the darkness.
Qʷo scnloʔ l' snlč'mintn.	You locked me in jail.
Łu miłχʷelstn č'u l' qʷoyeʔ.	The rest/peace is gone from me.

3. Čn č'upels łu t Sčč'masq't;
n'e pistem' n'em wičtn?
Ma! Šey' qʷo es t meʔmintm,
Yo! łu tł' kʷ'l'nč'meps!

3. I am lonesome for the heaven;
some day will I see it?
See! I am told to leave,
alas, from his door!

4. Łu skʷ'ʎ'usts łu t Kʷ'l'ncutn,
qʷo es wekʷłts. Qʷo es łc'ims.

ʔin xmenč łu Kʷ'l'ncutn,
u qʷo ʔaxeystm t ʔin šmen'.

4. The face of God,
he hides it from me. He is
punishing me.
I love God,
and he treated me like my
enemy.

5. Yesu Kʷi, ʔies nučmelsm.

Kʷmiʔ wičtn Mali!
T Yesu Kʷ'li, qʷo es ʔmensms.

T Mali qʷo mensmis.

5. Jesus Christ, I am wishing to
see him.
I wish I could see Mary!
Jesus Christ is turning his face
from me.
Mary turns her face from me.

6. Qʷo scnłepts łu t ʔi sxʷsixʷlt.

Qʷo scnłepts łu t ʔi sl'axt.

Miʔ ʔanwi qʷo nqʷn'mintxʷ,
kʷ, ʔi snkʷł qʷn'qʷeynt?

6. I have been forgotten by my
children.
I have been forgotten by my
friend.
Would you have pity on me,
you, my fellow pitiful one?

7. ʎ'e q'sip čnes n'loʔ.

N'em čn ʔocqeʔ n'e q'sip,
nełi ta qʷo es puʔsšitms,

nełi xemt łu ʔin xʷlxʷilt.

7. It has been a long time that I
have been imprisoned.
I will get out after a long time,
because nobody thinks about
me,
because heavy is my debt.

120

8. Miʔ čʼomistmnt łu qʼʷaylʼqs

n'e t nweymis snxʷuls
Yesu Kʷli łu čʼ Kʼʷlʼncutn,
ʔin xʷlxʷilt n'em nšƛ'pus?

8. Would you ask a favor of the Blackrobe
when he offers up the blood of Jesus Christ to God,
that my debt will be paid?

9. Qʷo es čawšt łu l'es łiqʼʷ.

Łu l' Mali, łu l' ʔin p'ҳot,
qʷo nq'eʔcišt łu l'es čacew's.

Šey' łu qeqł nmełistn.

9. You pray for me on the rosary.
In Mary, my parent,
you receive Holy Communion for me on Sundays.
That is what is going to be our peace/rest.

10. Kʷl' šol'ši u Kʷes nt'uk'ʷ,

kʷnew kʷ q'ʷeyłmist u kʷ ʔo.

U ҳʷl'stem' u ʔas čnweyl'sm

ʔa sl'aҳt es ʔulpmi?

10. If in the fire you were placed,
surely you would do your best to get out.
And why do you care so little for
your friend who is burning?

11. Kʷnl'op łu l'es nłoxʷ ʔa st'ma, ʔaqs ʔocqeʔm.
U ҳʷl'stem' u tas čn'šitxʷ

ʔa sl'aҳt u ʔan p'ҳot?

11. If into a hole your cow fell,
you would surely take it out.
And why do you not extend a hand
to your friend and elder parent?

12. Ta qʷo qes č ƛ'ʔič spuʔusent?

ʔaҳey n'e č ƛ'ʔič spuʔusmnct.

Pn' n'e qe nqʷn'miłt,
n'em n'qʷn'miłmn.

12. Do you not search my heart over?
It might be your heart that is searched later.
But if you have pity on us,
I will have pity on all of you.

Sl'aẋt

(Friend)

As sung by Joe Woodcock and others

This transcription is reproduced in color between pages 50 and 51.

The European origin of the above tune is unknown, but beyond the melodic glides infused through a process of musical indigenization, there is another feature common to the Native song style of the Columbia Plateau. Like "Qeqs Čšnim," "Sl'aẋt" utilizes what in Western terms might be defined as chromaticism in bars 10–12, introducing a note (A natural) that steps outside a standard key or pentatonic scale, characteristic of Columbia Plateau song forms. It is safe to assume that this note was not present in the original European tune but was added during the process of Native reinterpretation, which dramatically altered the character of the melody.

After the family visited the casket one last time, the body was taken by hearse to the mission church.[8] During the mass, hymns continued, sung in both Indian and Latin.[9] Upon conclusion of the mass, the casket was taken to the back of the church, and as friends and loved ones filed past the body in a line that trailed outdoors, Mitch and Mary would again offer "Sl'aẋt" (Friend), making a final appeal on behalf of the deceased for an unencumbered path to heaven (Connolly b). From there, the casket was carried to the cemetery, where Fr. Connolly would bless the gravesite and offer prayers. Michael then offered prayers in Salish, after which the body was lowered into the ground to an Indian hymn that begins, "[E]ternal rest grant unto them, O Lord" (Arlee n.d.:5; Connolly b). Johnny Arlee relays what came next, a practice rooted in a distinctly Native worldview:

> Immediately following, when the casket was lowered into the gravesite, if there are any little children from the immediate family of the deceased who were very close to the deceased, they would be handed across the open grave, always toward the east. Then the children would be led away from the grave to an awaiting car, or a distance away from the burial service. . . . The purpose for passing small children over the gravesite was said that sometimes a small child may miss this person, in searching, maybe crying in loneliness, possibly getting sick and eventually dying. Or, maybe the child would wake in the middle of the night screaming. Another reason was said that the spirit of the deceased was not at rest, so it needed company on his or her journey and as the young children were the most pure of heart without sin, they would be the ticket for them into happiness. So, for the sake of the bereaved family and the love of our little children, this practice was done. (Arlee n.d.:5)

Arlee continues, emphasizing the importance of giving the body back to Mother Earth as part of a cycle of birth and death: "At the completion of passing the children across the gravesite, a handful of dirt from everyone attending the burial service was thrown into the open grave. This signifies a reminder that man was created from clay of the earth, with a breath from God to give life and at death we return to the Mother Earth to become dust again" (Arlee n.d.:5).

After the funeral, people returned to the home, hall, or longhouse where the wake was held for the memorial lunch or dinner, followed by a giveaway. In the past, memorial feasts and giveaways took place up to a year after the funeral. They have since become condensed, a matter of convenience in a more time-intensive age. When the immediate family had returned from the gravesite, Michael would ask everyone to face the site where the body lay during the wake, after which he offered a prayer for the foods (Arlee n.d.:6). The feast consisted primarily of traditional foods (as it does today), including camas, bitterroot, boiled black moss, venison, and huckleberries. Out of respect for foods given by the Creator, what was not taken into the body was taken home, in bags, jars, and boxes.

Following the feast the tables were cleared, making room for the giveaway. In addition to all the earthly possessions of the deceased, the family purchased items such as blankets, scarves, and yard goods, all of which were placed on a blanket in the center of the room. Before the giveaway, Michael would offer a prayer, opening the floor for other speakers to give final words on behalf of the deceased for all within the community to hear: "After the speakers were finished, the rosary was recited and hymns were sung. When this was finished, whoever was in charge of the giveaway was handed a set of clothing which the deceased wore. This was shown to the people and explained that this was what the person had worn on the last days of his or her life on earth. Then the tears are open to be shed for the bereaving family and friends of the deceased" (Arlee n.d.:8).

The primary function of a giveaway in the context of a wake is twofold. While removing potentially painful reminders of the deceased from the family home, the items also serve as important reminders in the community, contributing to a collective memory of the individual that will live on. The giveaway is also seen as an important part of letting go, not just for friends and family but for the soul of the deceased, freed of material ties that threaten to keep it anchored to earth.

After the last items of clothing worn by the deceased were given to a family member or close friend, the other items were distributed, each earmarked for a specific person. When all had been given Michael would offer one last prayer, and with that the wake, like the life it honored, was officially put to rest. Through his participation in the Indian wakes, Connolly gradually adopted Native cultural and spiritual ways of knowing—lessons learned through commiseration with the living and the dead. The wake was his entry point into an ethos of indigeneity created by the Native community, allowing him to be conversant in a collaborative venture with his "two Indian grandfathers," in which that ethos of indigeneity was brought to the Catholic mass.

The Indian Mass

In 1850, eight years after the founding of the first Catholic mission among the Coeur d'Alene, they built a church overlooking the Coeur d'Alene River that extended skyward as if reaching for the hand of God. Erected from timbers found throughout Coeur d'Alene lands, the church was a grand gesture in honor of a new religion. Those lands would eventually be pared down by the federal government, rendering the church an orphan left to fend for itself outside the boundaries of the reservation in 1876.[10] Every year on August 15, Mitch and Mary Michael would join other Catholic Coeur d'Alene for the annual celebration to commemorate the building of the mission their relatives were forced to leave behind, participating in a procession and taking in oral accounts in the form of a dramatic play. By doing so they both reified and reaffirmed a faith that, for the Coeur d'Alene, was rooted in the intertwined stories of Circling Raven, the Coeur d'Alene, and the Blackrobes. At one such celebration in the late 1960s, Michael sang the "Scho-chowm" prayer song during the seminal procession from the church to the cemetery below. Months before, Michael had suggested to Fr. Cornelius Byrne that the "Scho-chowm" prayer song would be appropriate because of its general application in the context of a traditional indigenous ceremony to give thanks for food. Connolly witnessed the procession that year and credited Michael's innovation with teaching him "how to incorporate some aspects of traditional Indian ritual into the Catholic mass" (Connolly b). The "Scho-chowm" prayer song was one of many Native elements that soon found their way into a retooled Catholic mass, each a quiet victory for Indian people who for generations had patiently awaited a mass in which they could recognize—among the vestments, the linens, the altar, and the cross—an undeniable aura of Indianness.

Mitch and Mary Michael standing at a monument to Fr. Joseph Cataldo at the site of his first mission, located in the present-day city of Spokane.

Soon after Gibson Eli was baptized, he contributed to the efforts of Connolly and Michael to indigenize the mass. The Indian Center in Spokane became an incubator within which they refashioned the Christmas midnight mass, changing its constitution at a molecular level. With drums in hand, Michael and Eli opened with a Native blessing song, leading a procession of participants into the area where the mass would be held. After the offering of bread and wine came Eli, Michael, and Connolly's most bold and innovative contribution: the Cup Dance. Stemming from the use of the traditional "Scho-chowm" prayer song that Michael had introduced at the August 15 celebration a few years before, they went much further, adapting elements of the traditional ceremony in which the song appeared. In addition to a Native song, the mass now included its ancient corollary, Native dance. Making its Catholic debut at a large diocesan-wide mass at the Spokane Coliseum, it was unlike any mass those in attendance had ever seen. As the "Scho-chowm" prayer song began, three boys holding eagle fans and dressed in traditional regalia knelt on one knee, facing the altar. The introduction of the song, like the sections between each verse, consisted of an elongated melody sung by Michael and Eli over the free-metered rumbling of the drum. As the drum transitioned to a steady, upbeat pattern and the song settled into place, the boys began dancing to and from the altar, returning to a kneeling position between verses (Connolly

Gibson Eli and Mitch Michael singing together.

c). During the final verse, the boys danced in a circle around the altar, honoring the foods and the body and blood of Jesus with tools passed down through the generations, age-old technologies used long before indigenous Columbia Plateau peoples had ever heard the Blackrobes utter his name.

In addition to the "Scho-chowm" prayer song and Cup Dance, Michael, Eli, and Connolly brought "Qeqs npiyelsi" (We Are Going to Be Happy), the "shaking hands song," into the indigenized mass. Directly following the mass, with Connolly standing in front of the altar, Mitch would start the song, shake Connolly's hand, and stand beside him. Eli was next, followed by members of the congregation. Everyone sang in unison, and as each person extended his or her hand—first to the priest and then down the line—a circle slowly began to form. More than symbolic, the circle, through touch, prayer, and song, actively solidified and strengthened communal bonds that would live beyond the boundaries of the mass itself (Connolly c).

Virginia Matt recalls "Qeqs npiyelsi" and other Indian hymns in the context of New Year's sleigh rides she took as a child, during which her mother and father (Mary and Mitch Michael) would carve tracks in the snow as they went from one house to the next. In the process they created miles of communal threads that would remain long after the snow had melted. As they approached each home along the way, they sang the hymn with a growing chorus that swelled with every stop, filling the night sky with sounds of Salish that echoed Native voices of centuries past.

> I could remember going around . . . Dad used to get the horses on the sleigh and when he'd start doing that, oh, *God*, we were just tickled we were going to ride on the sleigh that night. He'd put bells on all over and he'd hang lanterns, three on one side and three on the other. He'd cover us all up and him and Mom, they'd sit up front and we could hear them while we were under there nice and warm. They'd be *singin'* Christmas carols and first we'd get to Grandma's and then we'd all jump out and go in there. Then after a little while we'd all come out and then she'd be getting in with us. Then we'd go on to Catherine Finley's house and from there to Martha Sherwood's house. Then she'd get dressed and get on the sleigh with us. Then we'd cross the highway and go across the creek there to Ellen Pierre's place. Her and her husband used to get on. My *goodness*, we'd have a sleigh full . . . Then we'd go over the little hill and go to Lucy Finley's. After her and her husband got ready, then mom would take us and move us all right up behind them so there'd be room for more. Then we used to go on down the road to Ignace William's place and go around this other way and go down to Maggie Adam's. Then we'd go down the road and head back toward Worley. My goodness, by *that* time we were *asleep*! I don't know how long it took to do that . . . We'd get back to the house and then they'd all get off and get into the house and they'd all be sittin' at the table eatin'. We'd all go right to *bed*; it was such a *long* ride.
>
> (Hamill interview, July 23, 2009)

Qeqs npiyelsi
(We Are Going to Be Happy)

Qeqs npiyelsi, šey' qeqs nkʷnem.	We are going to be happy, we are going to sing.
Qeqs npiyelsi, šey'qeqs nkʷnem.	We are going to be happy, we are going to sing.
K'ʷl'ncutn sqʷseʔs,	God's son,
x̣ʷl' sqʷn'qʷeynt łu sqelixʷ,	because pitiful are the people,
tl' nwist cwamist.	from above he came quickly.
Cwełkʷup, x̣est Yesu.	He came down, good Jesus.

Qeqs npiyelsi
(We Are Going to Be Happy)

As sung by Johnny Arlee

This transcription is reproduced in color between pages 50 and 51.

After its debut at the diocesan-wide mass at the Spokane Coliseum, Eli, Michael, and Connolly brought the indigenized mass to the Indian Center in Spokane in the form of a Christmas mass. In addition to changes in song and ritual, their version of the Christmas mass included a nativity scene with indigenized figures of Jesus, Mary, and Joseph adorned in Native regalia and seated inside a tepee. Draped behind them was a painted canvas, upon which images of animals, the sacred sweathouse, and angelic drummers appeared (Connolly c).[11] As a whole, the nativity scene, a static statement as referentially rich as da Vinci's *The Last Supper*, represented a comprehensive contextual shift in which Catholicism was indigenized, transferred, and transformed into a framework that embodied Native ontologies.

The inclusion of animals highlights the role of animal spirits in Native Columbia Plateau communities, where one's relevance and status were dependent on one's ability to bond with an animal spirit. Animal spirits were a part of every spiritual concern or event, whether in the context of personal prayer, collective ceremony, or private healing. The drummers reflect the integral role of song in Native communities, in which an event of any consequence would be met with song. Placing them at the birth of Jesus serves as an endorsement of sorts—a way of conveying the event's significance to Native Christians still rooted in age-old traditions. The sweathouse, like the churches introduced by missionaries in the nineteenth century, had always been a place of worship and prayer. It was the original "church" of indigenous Plateau peoples, so potent and

Indian Christmas Scene, Sacred Heart Mission, De Smet, Idaho.

effective as a delivery system for power and prayer that it has survived all attempts to eradicate it.[12]

Christmas mass at the Indian Center also included a "Blackrobe" altar covered with a black blanket that was given to Connolly during his Spokane, Kalispel, and Coeur d'Alene Indian naming ceremony. It featured a beaded "IHS" insignia adorned with three eagle feathers. Representing the Holy Trinity, the three feathers constitute more than simple metaphor. As the highest-flying bird, eagles spend much of their time on the edge of heaven, offering strong medicine that is invariably positive and pure. Placing eagle feathers on the altar brought it to life, infusing the Indian mass with spiritual power that would lift the prayers skyward.

Plateau tribes have seen their share of Native prophets. Recasting Jesus within the mold of their spiritual traditions, beyond emphasizing points of resonance with Catholicism, expresses two related truths held by indigenous Plateau Christians: (1) Our traditional spiritual ways are valid and (2) Jesus—as a powerful prophet—would have agreed. The early Blackrobes clearly did not, and they went to great lengths to stifle Native spiritual traditions in the Plateau. Through the efforts of Michael, Eli, and Connolly, Native Catholics were becoming free to lend their voice to a dialogue their ancestors had been unable to have, one that took over a century to begin. They were bringing the spiritual scales of history closer to balance, succeeding where the Jesuits had failed. Not content to stop with the Christmas mass at the Indian Center in Spokane, Michael, Eli, and Connolly took the Indian mass to annual powwows on the Spokane, Flathead, Kalispel, and Coeur d'Alene reservations. The following is an outline of the Indian mass they developed, in which the comprehensive effects of Catholic indigenization are evident.

1. Procession:

Priests and helpers enter and form a "sacred circle" to the song "Jesuit," which came to Francis SiJohn (Spokan) in a dream. People in attendance get up from their seats and join a circular procession around the altar behind the cross and eagle staff, following Jesus in an Indian way, making holy the inner circle and leaving outside of it all other thoughts and problems by focusing on the sacred within the circle.

2. Opening Prayer

3. Holy Water

4. Bible Readings and the Gospel:
Bible readings and commentary blending the teachings of Jesus with the ancient teachings of the ancestors. Accompanied by a drum.

5. Four Direction Prayer:
Sun rising (east), warmth (south), cold rains (north), sun setting and rest (west). Prayer accompanied by the burning of sage (smudging).

6. Bread and Wine

7. Proclamation of Faith:
Cup Dance, includes altar dance to the "Scho-chowm" prayer song to give thanks for food.

8. The Lord's Prayer:
In Salish with Native sign language.

9. Communion:
In Salish with Indian hymn "Always, always I will love you."

10. Closing Prayer/Blessing:
"Qeqs npiyelsi" (shake hands song), in a circle, "Let's be happy and rejoice." Everyone comes to the altar and shakes hands with everyone else, forming a large circle in the process that signifies unity with Jesus and one another.

Together, Gibson Eli, Fr. Connolly, and Mitch Michael forged a path through the thicket of history, where the thorns of religious ideology that divided people by denomination gave way to cooperation, unity, and respect. The religious adaptation that took root in the Reductions and found a place in DeSmet's mission was concerned with conversion, not conversation. While Connolly became conversant in the language of the Indian wake and the medicine dance, Michael and Eli found new avenues for Native expression in the Catholic mass. Song was their primary modus operandi. Egalitarian in their approach, they embarked on a collective search for the sacred in which the dark shadows cast by the Blackrobes a century before were momentarily lifted, disappearing in an unfamiliar flash of spiritual symbiosis never before seen in the Columbia Plateau. Like a shooting star igniting the heavens it would fall to earth, and although Connolly's two Indian grandfathers would soon drift out of sight, elements of their work remained, embedded in fertile soil awaiting new growth.

7

The End and the Afterlife

On a beautiful summer day in July 1972, Mitch and Mary Michael's world came crashing down around them. They had just returned from White Swan on the Yakama reservation, where they were celebrating the Fourth of July with family and friends. Their grandson, Jackson Alexander, told Mitch Michael he was going to the courts with some friends to play basketball. Instead of shooting hoops, the boys went to Rocky Point on Lake Coeur d'Alene. While swimming Jackson became fatigued and began to panic. As he struggled, his brother grabbed hold of him but was forced to let go for fear that he might drown along with him. Upon hearing the news of Jackson's drowning, members of the family began assembling at the home of Lavinia (Jackson's mother), a place from which to weather the disaster, collect whatever emotional remnants remained, and begin building again. After everyone arrived, Mitch called his children to the back room. He had something to say:

> Now I tell you, my children, do what is right. We no longer have any elders to talk to us, or tell us what to do at this wake. I looked around and didn't see no speaker around to ask what this word means. All the speakers use this word: *Qw'nqw'ntsutn.* I'm going to tell you children what this word means: "we're pitiful, it can't be helped." But it *can* be helped. It is us, the old people that have children, that can stop it by correcting their children. We are the parents. We are to blame. We should talk to our children; tell them what is right and what is wrong. Now all of you, my children, take care of *your children.* Never leave your children. Take them wherever you go. This all comes back to me and I no longer can take it. This is the last time you will hear me.[1]

Upon finishing his talk, Mitch collapsed. Moments later, his heart surrendered to sorrow that had become too much to bear, freeing his spirit from this earth and the persistent pain that came with being Indian.

It was standing room only at the joint wake for Michael and his grandson, held at the mission church in De Smet. Family members representing the hundreds of people Michael had sung into the afterlife came to honor him—there to support his family in the same way they had been supported. The community had lost one of its great prayer leaders, among the last of a generation able to bring a precontact indigenous identity into an imported faith—able to weave disparate worlds into one. Connolly was one of his beneficiaries, fortunate to have stood by Michael's side for years as a fellow arbiter of the afterlife. Connolly had been to innumerable wakes, had conducted countless funerals in Native communities where transcendence and tragedy walked hand in hand. No amount of experience could have prepared him to bury his mentor, however, a "grandfather" with whom he shared a bond more intimate than that of father and son, stretching from the familial into the sacred. Standing over Mitch's coffin, Connolly gently placed in his hands a crucifix he had received during his first vows as a Jesuit in 1951. With tears in his eyes, he asked Mitch to keep praying for him, hoping the crucifix might act as a bridge to bring them together again one day.

For the next eight years, Connolly continued to accompany Gibson Eli to healings throughout the Columbia Plateau and Canada, a period in which Eli was at the height of his powers. Calls came from far and wide, and Eli rarely said no. During this period his health began to wane, seeming to decrease in direct proportion to his growing spiritual power, as if his spirit were being coaxed from his body. Before Eli's initial heart attack word had gotten out that his health was failing, and those who loved him while living sought to ease him through death. Eli recalls their first effort to bring him home:

> I went to sleep and at once I dreamed, and here was my wife, just like if I was awake, standing right before my bed. She said, "You're pitiful, I'm going to take you home." So I looked at

her just like I was awake. She had her hands out like this, so I turned around to grab her hands, and somebody screamed and screamed. And I looked back, and here was my little grandson, just like I was going away and leaving him in a store or something, the way he screamed and jumped around. So I turned around to grab his hand to go. When I turned around, I looked—my wife was way out there just like behind a cloud standing there. Soon as I looked, she turned around. When I woke up, I couldn't get my breath. I started hitting my fists . . . and then thought if I can just get to the door the kids would hear me call. I just got to the door and tried to holler, but I couldn't holler, just standing there. I kind of came to, but it was quite a while before I got my breath. I finally laid down, and the next morning they took me to the hospital.[2]

Sometime after he regained his strength and got back on his feet, Eli was visited by his mother and grandfather in a dream. As they smiled at him lovingly, his mother said, "Son, we're after you." Eli turned to his grandfather, who likewise said, "Grandson, we're after you." As he grabbed their hands he woke to find his heart racing in his chest. He felt sick the rest of the day and thought another heart attack might come at any time. Against the advice of those closest to him, Eli continued to conduct healings, confronted with the irony that while he extracted various maladies from the bodies of others, he could not heal his own heart. He had been staying with his niece for some time when, on the morning of July 20, 1980, he called Connolly at De Smet. Things were hectic at the mission that day, and after a brief conversation Connolly told Eli he would call him back later. About noon, Connolly received a call from Eli's niece. She informed him that Eli had quietly passed while sitting in a chair next to the phone, waiting for his call.

After Eli's passing, the healings continued. About a year and a half after his death, Eli's niece became very ill, so ill that she lost her desire to live. Tired and sick, she climbed the stairs and entered his old room. Feeling isolated by her illness, she lay down on his bed to be close to him.

As she drifted off to sleep she found him standing over her, accompanied by a man on either side wearing a long white robe. Eli asked each of them to remove an item from the bed. One removed a white blanket and the other a section of brown plaid cloth. He then told his niece, "You will be well now." The next day, she was.[3]

After Michael's and Eli's passings, the legacy they established with Connolly in the form of the Indian mass continued, representative of a Native community that after over a century of waiting had reached the spiritual middle ground they had sought from the beginning. But change was on the horizon. Subsequent generations were becoming less and less interested, perhaps viewing the middle ground of Indian Catholicism as another site of surrender, *lost ground* to the colonial enterprise that had taken just about everything. As is the case today, elders were passing away without passing on tradition. Without younger people to take up the mantle, prayer leaders and medicine people were becoming few and far between. The generation of Eli and Michael still had direct lineal ties to a precolonial past, and their understanding of that world enabled them to walk into a Catholic sphere grounded, steadfast, and sure. They viewed the spiritual options before them not as contradictory but complementary, a view that perhaps appears naïve to younger generations, who without the benefit of their elders' perspectives are left to draw their own conclusions. For them the technology-driven values of the outside world everywhere encroach, like the final vestiges of a colonial enterprise determined to finish the job. Meanwhile, the infrastructure that supported prayer leaders and medicine people continues to give way, accompanied by a pronounced material poverty, ills that past generations, regardless of their spiritual orientation or power, were unable to cure. Less informed and more rigid, young Native people overall have adopted a narrower view than their forebears, unable perhaps to see how the promise of heavenly salvation will bring them a better life here on earth. It begs the question: How is this story relevant to them?

Accompanying the material poverty in Native Plateau communities is a poverty of self. At no time since the beginning of the colonial conquest in North America has the struggle over identity seemed greater than with today's younger generation in Indian Country. The evidence suggests that for Mitch Michael, Gibson Eli, and their contemporaries, Indian Catholicism, rather than creating a crisis of identity, broadened and strengthened their Native sense of self. Drawing on a legacy established by the early Native pioneers who explored the foreign terrain of Catholicism, they continued the process of indigenization, finding strength and empowerment in the process. The story of Eli, Michael, and their contemporaries, while historically recent, has largely been lost to the generations of their grandchildren and great-grandchildren. It is my hope that this book will help bring the story back. Reading about the sacred adventures of Michael, Eli, and Connolly might serve to make the members of the younger generations a little less rigid, demonstrating that identity, as a process of self-definition, resists conforming to casual conceptions of Indianness (or, for that matter, Jesuitness). In their spiritual lives Eli, Michael, and Connolly were concerned with seeking the sacred, a quest that brought the prayer leader, the Jesuit, and the medicine man together in a common cause. Their quest falls outside the black and white bookends of history, where stories of cultural collision and conflict are abundant and easy to find.

The academic audience for this book may find this story just as challenging. In the opening chapters I suggest that the standard tools of scientific inquiry would be insufficient to explore this story's central touchstone—song and its relationship to spiritual power. I dispensed with "ineffective intellectual methodologies" (Trafzer 1986:x) in pursuit of this relationship, embracing Native epistemologies while calling for a paradigmatic shift in approach, away from the solid stuff of science to a Native spiritual reality. I have avoided engaging in what Adam Gaudry has termed "extraction research" (2011:113), in which cultural knowledge of value to Native communities is taken for the sole benefit of the academic enterprise and is decontextualized, ripped from its source and left to languish in the pages, conference halls, and classrooms of academic discourse. For a book published by an academic press under the banner of an academic discipline, this is admittedly a tall order. Fortunately, the disciplines with which it is most closely aligned are, in my view, sympathetic to its position and approach. Native American and indigenous studies privilege an inside perspective, often eschewing Western ways of knowing, which have proven inadequate to the task of grasping indigenous ontologies. The disciplines embrace an ongoing dialogue with communities with which they are engaged, often employing community-based approaches to research in which the community stands to benefit from the results. Ethnomusicology (my own disciplinary "home") is concerned with people and music, approaching the study of music as a component of—or simply *as*— culture. Ethnomusicologists often work directly with communities to preserve and perpetuate indigenous traditions, projects that in many cases move well beyond music into the realm of advocacy and activism. Although I believe ethnomusicology can readily accommodate this Native-centered approach (as I indicate in chapter 4), the discipline as a whole has not as yet contended in any substantive way with phenomena integral to the health and vitality of Native communities: song and spirituality.

An Expanding Field

The founders of the emerging field of ethnomusicology envisioned an inclusive field that would enable researchers to examine music from many different angles. At a meeting of the American Anthropological Association in Philadelphia in 1952, Alan Merriam suggested to Willard Rhodes that they launch a musicological society "that would bring together sociologists, statisticians, acousticians, musicologists, ethnologists, dance ethnographers, linguists, folk electrical engineers, psychologists, and theologians. And doubtless quite a few others" (McAllester 2006:200). Merriam and Rhodes, along with David McAllester and Charles Seeger, recognized the need to move beyond the field of musicology, which was unapologetically geared toward historical aspects of Western classical tradition. They also recognized that multiple perspectives would be required to understand the multifaceted nature of music.

There can be no denying that anthropology, Merriam's primary field of study, has loomed large in ethnomusicology. From the beginning, the search for ethnomusicological theories has led ethnomusicologists repeatedly to its door. Indeed, in any analysis of musical expression, one cannot get very far without bumping into questions of culture—anthropology's intellectual domain. Accounts of spiritual phenomena throughout this book reference culture and in most cases suggest some level of cultural codification. Still, I view the foregoing as more of a spiritual study than a cultural one. And while it is fundamentally concerned with song, I would be reluctant to settle for the term *musical*. Musical studies typically deal with musical constructions, offering little in terms of exploring song's function within the whole of spiritual experience. Song used within a ceremonial context to facilitate power may sound like music, it may feel like music, but for all intents and purposes, it is not "music." Sound structures in ceremony are beholden to spiritual phenomena. Without such phenomena, sound becomes meaningless, a meandering and isolated element severed from its source.

In the preceding pages I endeavor to understand song, not as an isolated thing called music or strictly as a component of culture, but as a force that when functioning in tandem with power can transcend as well as transform the mundane world. To understand power requires a foray into the ontology of experience, illuminated through the experience of the individual. Scholars focused on such experience perhaps owe a debt of gratitude to the pioneers of ethnomusicology, who in the early 1950s suggested that studies into the limitless nature of music ought to proceed without limitations. Although ethnomusicology is perhaps less interdisciplinary than its founders envisioned, ethnomusicologists tacitly accept their freedom to pursue any thread tied to music. While examining song and power I have taken advantage of this freedom, letting go of standard musicological and anthropological conventions in pursuit of sounds—in Native terms—that constitute the sacred.

As the cornerstone of ethnomusicology, fieldwork is considered an essential component of any substantive ethnomusicological study. In the beginning, preoccupied with documenting musical cultures that had yet to be recorded or written about, ethnomusicologists typically travelled to far-flung locales to conduct fieldwork. While ethnomusicologists still clock considerable miles crisscrossing the planet, many studies have shifted closer to home, with fieldwork increasingly taking place in an ethnomusicologist's "own backyard" (Nettl 2005:186). Ethnomusicological studies have also become increasingly collaborative, as many ethnomusicologists have chosen to work directly with cultural insiders (in cases where they are not) who, rather than being "informants," have become co-*authors*. At the same time, ethnomusicological studies have taken a turn toward the internal. Through pathways such as ethnography of the individual, reflexivity, and musical experience, ethnomusicologists have examined inner processes that contribute to musical performance, embodiment, and understanding. It might be said that in the process of gathering information for this book, the "field" consisted of the spiritual continuum and the realm of spirit. Central to Gibson Eli's story are his *sumesh,* or animal spirits. Like any other "source," they had much to contribute, teaching us about a sphere seldom seen or heard. Just as traditional ethnomusicological fieldwork often takes place in a shared space where people gather to interact, these interactions take place within the spiritual continuum, a gathering place for people and spirits. In the twenty-first century, ethnomusicological fieldwork can happen anywhere, from an external geographic locale to the interior realm of the mind and spirit. It therefore seems logical to consider the spiritual continuum as valid a location as any for further fieldwork and research.

Admittedly, options for such fieldwork are more limited in the Columbia Plateau than they were two hundred (or even twenty) years ago. The spiritual phenomena with which Eli engaged as "the last medicine man of the Spokan tribe" appear to be on the decline, as collective spaces and personal channels for such engagement have been reduced. Moreover, while such phenomena continue, they are seldom discussed, remaining an intensely personal matter for individuals who are wary of prying eyes. Spiritual leaders I have worked with in the Columbia Plateau find themselves in a "catch-22," lamenting that spiritual traditions are being lost to their young people. I have labored to strike a balance in the preceding pages, relaying facets of accounts that may be of value to future generations without giving away details better left within the spiritual sphere.

Despite a decline, there is plenty of evidence that the channels to the spirit realm, where the spirits seem to be patiently awaiting a resurgence of interest, are still open. Although not great in numbers, young people *are* participating, and the songs and visions continue to come. Rather than simply echoing a past forever out of reach, they ring with relevance and truth in the present, just like the prescient prophecies of the eighteenth and nineteenth centuries. During the course of fieldwork in 2007, I met with a woman who had such a dream, one with a timely message for Fr. Connolly:

> I come home and we cleaned huckleberries all day and was tired, so I went to bed. My grandson just went to live with my niece because his mom wasn't able to care for him . . . She's goin' to school. So we found a good place for him, he's got special needs. I was *really* lonesome for him—because he's been living with us. So, in my *dream* we were livin' in this apartment and there was a rap on the door and "Oh!" Because it was only two bedrooms and I had *five* kids in that two bedroom. We were just *wall-to-wall* beds and I thought, "Oh, God, who's coming? It's going to be a *mess*." So I opened up the door and here was Robert Sherwood [a close friend of Connolly and Eli]! And he'd *never* come in my dream before. He said, "Gib said we gotta pick you up, you're worried about a baby. We gotta go check that baby out." I said, "Okay, let me go get my shoes," and he said, "Oh, no, you don't need shoes, just come on." So I just had my slippers and away I went. I looked at that station wagon and my heart started beatin' really fast 'cause in my dream it's one of those old station wagons with . . . it looks like paneling on the sides, you know. And I thought, "Oh, God, it doesn't have no seatbelts so let him drive real safe." [Eli

rarely drove with all four wheels on the ground.] So I get in and close the door and ZZOOOM! And we're just goin' and there's rocks spittin' out and I'm thinkin', "We'll make it, I know we'll make it, I'll just *pray*." So I put my head down and I was prayin' and I was listenin' to them talkin' and Robert said, "You know, Fr. Connolly's really worried." And Gibson said, "Yeah, I seen that he's worried." He said, "Well, he doesn't have to worry." And I said, "What's he worried about?" And Gib said, "Yeah, he's worried because all of his friends are leaving this world and he thinks that maybe he missed his time or his time is coming up." And Robert said, "Oh, no, he didn't miss anything yet. He's still got work to do. There's still *sinners* out there!" and then Gib started laughing and he said, "He knows what sinners go through! When it's his time we'll go pick him up, Robert. That will make his journey easier." Robert said, "Yeah, you can drive." I'm thinkin', "Oh my god! Please don't let him drive!" So we pull in front of my cousin's house and I'd never been to her house before. And here is this brown . . . it looks like a really old house and I'm thinkin', "Well, gosh, I don't know if she stays *here*." Robert said, "Yeah, baby's inside, just go in," he said. "They're sleepin'." He said, "Check out the baby and see his room, make sure everything is to your liking," he said, "and you come back and we'll head home." So I get back, I go in there and I see he's just sleeping really peaceful, his room is just nice and he's got a nice *bed* and he's got new *pajamas* on. Oh, I just felt so much better and I kissed him on the cheek and I went out and still had my slippers . . . I left a slipper on the porch and I put it back on and Gib said, "Come on, we don't got all night, we have work yet to do!" [*laughter*] And I thought, "Oh, God, please just help me make it home." So I got in the car . . . I'm not kiddin', it seems like you just get in the car and you get to ride for about 5 minutes! [*laughter*] So I get back in the car and then he turned and he looked at me, and he said, "You need to tell Father Connolly to quit worryin'. When it comes his time, Robert and I are going to come pick him up. He won't have no stops; we'll make sure he gets right to the other side." (Hamill interview, March 3, 2007)

Soon after hearing some of the details of the dream, Connolly shared with me that he felt this book was the "work" left to be done, and when it is finished, he hopes to join his two Indian grandfathers on a rough-and-tumble ride into the afterlife.

Notes

Preface

1. The Niimiipuu are more commonly known and referred to as the Nez Perce. For the purposes of this study, I have chosen their precolonial name, which translates as "the People" (Aoki 1994:489). Like many such colonial names, the Nez Perce have adopted a term ascribed to them, in this case a French phrase meaning "pierced nose." The term was a misnomer, as the Niimiipuu did not in fact pierce their noses.
2. "Spokan," as opposed to "Spokane," is the preferred spelling among many of the Spokan people, who also refer to themselves as "Spokani."
3. Held in winter throughout the Columbia Plateau, the medicine dance has been integral to the lifeways of indigenous Plateau people for centuries.

Introduction

1. For a cultural cross section of studies that explore the relationship between song and spiritual power, see Berliner 1978; Feld 1982; Seeger 1987; Nettl 1989; Friedson 1996; Marett 2005; Hamill 2008; Jankowsky 2010.
2. The Salish people of northwestern Montana have been referred to variously as Flathead, Flathead-Salish, and Salish. Although the origin of the term remains elusive, by all accounts "Flathead" was a misnomer perpetuated by early trappers and explorers (Partoll 1951). Like many other erroneous appellations ascribed to tribes, the term "Flathead" stuck, adopted as the official name for the tribe and reservation. I have chosen to use "Salish," the operative term among the People prior to contact and the preferred term among many tribal members today.
3. As a blending of cultural and religious elements, this may strike many as a clear case of syncretism or hybridity. In my view, the concepts of *syncretism* and *hybridity* are problematic, and I have chosen to avoid the terms here. For more, see *Syncretism in Religion* (Leopold and Jensen 2005) and "Theorizing the Hybrid" (Kapchan and Strong 1999).
4. The figure of 370 million comes from *State of the World's Indigenous Peoples* (Stamatopoulou 2009). For a concise history of the global indigenous movement, including the role of the International Labor Organization and the United Nations, see Niezen 2003.

Chapter 1. Power and Prophecy in the Plateau

1. Similar prophetic experiences characterized by stressful events can be found throughout the Bible. In one such account, "The Hebrew Prophet Joel, in a time of great distress, warned the Israelites to turn away from sin. A plague of locusts was ravaging the land; the day of

the Lord's wrath was approaching. If the people gathered, repented, and renewed their covenant with the Almighty, however, Joel assured them that bounty would again reign in Zion. God, speaking through his early surrogate, warranted that for the chosen people, having returned to righteousness, 'I will pour out my spirit upon all flesh; and your sons and your daughters shall prophesy, your old men shall dream dreams, and your young men shall see visions'" (Moses 1985:335).

2. "Pom-pom" is another term for the Washat, a ceremony held throughout the Columbia Plateau. The term refers specifically to the handheld drums utilized in Washat ceremonies.

3. The Wanapum people occupy an area on the Columbia River referred to as Priest Rapids and are members of the Confederated Tribes of the Yakama Nation. The Wanapum term for their homeland is P'na.

4. The term *dream*, as it is used here, can be misleading. The dream described in Luls's accounts is not of the ordinary variety routinely experienced during sleep but differs in clarity and quality. These differences are easily discerned by the individual, as a "dream" such as the one experienced by Luls is as vivid as what one may experience while awake. In Account 1, Luls does not appear to make a distinction between his dream and his waking state, saddened as he is that the "holy people . . . almost came down to . . . where we live." I use the term *dream* for the sake of consistency in this volume when it has been used in a referenced account but opt for the term *vision* whenever possible, as it more accurately represents the lucid quality of the phenomenon.

5. Accounts of death experiences can be found in many cultures throughout the world. For cross-cultural research on the death experience, including studies on what is termed the "near-death experience" (NDE) in the West, see Moody 1977; Ring 1984; Fenske 1990; Ring and Valarino 1998; Bailey 2001; and Beck and Colli 2003.

6. By "them," Hununwe is referring to spirits that are present in the ceremony and occupy the realm of spirit.

7. The wars over dams and salmon have been ongoing for much of the twentieth century in the Plateau. See Walker 1967; Harden 1996; and Aguilar 2005.

8. The Dawes Act forced Native American families and individuals within reservations onto allotments, at which time the remainder of reservation lands were opened to Euro-American settlement. By opening Native territories to settlement through what amounted to a large-scale land grab, its authors hoped Native peoples would gently assimilate into the lifeways of the colonizers, a notion that was as naïve as it was devastating to Native communities.

9. According to the Wilkes account, the vision would have occurred around 1791.

10. Verne Ray gives the period as somewhere "in the latter part of the eighteenth or early part of the nineteenth century" (1933:108). The "book" arrived with missionaries, who first settled in the Plateau in the

mid-1830s (Walker 1985:39–40). Spokan Garry, who attended the Red River mission school in Winnipeg, Manitoba, Canada, is said to have brought a Bible back to the Spokan upon his return in 1830. Soon after, in 1831, the previously mentioned "Nez Perce–Flathead" delegation set out for St. Louis in search of missionaries who might furnish the book and illuminate its teachings, a journey that may have been motivated in part by Spokan Garry's possession of the Bible and knowledge of its contents (Drury 1936:76–79). The subsequent arrival of the Bible in the Plateau, firmly in the hands of missionaries, can be seen as a critical step in the manifestation of Silimxnotylmilakabok's prophecy, in which "a different kind of man" from the East carrying a book would signal the beginning of the end for the indigenous Plateau world.

11. Following Garry and Pelly, five other boys from Columbia Plateau tribes (two Niimiipuu and one each from the Cayuse, Spokan, and Kutenai tribes) were sent to the Red River school in 1830. Spokan Berens died while attending the school, and Kutenai Collins died shortly after returning home in 1833. The three remaining boys—Ellice, Pitt (both Niimiipuu), and Cayuse Halket (Cayuse)—were well known but less influential than Pelly and Garry (Josephy 1965:88–89).

12. *Ipnú·cilí·lpt* was a derogatory term used by missionaries and Christian Indian converts to describe ceremonies in which circular turning was a prominent feature (L. Olsen, pers. comm.).

13. *Sumesh* is the Salish term for spirit guardian or helper.

Chapter 2. Christians Answer the Call

1. Many religious scholars remain dissatisfied with the term "Counter-Reformation," which frames the activities within the Catholic Church during the period from 1545 to 1648 simply as a reaction to the Protestant Reformation. While reclaiming papal authority was an absolute priority during a period in which "Catholic emperors and princes captured and recatholicized territories hitherto under the banner of Protestant reform" (Hsia 2005:2), it also consisted of an "evolutionary adaptation of the Catholic religion and of the Catholic Church to new forces" (Evennett in Hsia 2005:3). In the end, the Counter-Reformation might be best viewed as a spectrum characterized by spiritual renewal on the one end and ecclesiastical control on the other (Brockey 2007:10). For a compelling argument in favor of the more encompassing term "Early Modern Catholicism," see O'Malley 2000.

2. The peoples who became collectively known as the Guaraní were not a homogenous group at the point of contact with Europeans; they lived in independent villages, speaking different dialects of what has been labeled the Tupi-Guaraní language. Prior to contact they referred to themselves as *abá* (men) or *ñande or* (all of us) but eventually adopted the term used by Europeans, Guaraní, a word meaning "warrior" in their language (Ganson 2003:18). When the Europeans arrived in the

sixteenth century, the Guaraní occupied the Atlantic coast of South America from Barra de Cananea to Rio Grande do Sul and up the Paraná, Uruguay, and Paraguay rivers, including the islands of the Río de la Plata (Métraux in Steward 1963:69).

3. As used in the seventeenth century, the term was not defined as a "reduction" in the contemporary sense. Stemming from the Latin verb *reducere* ("to lead back or together"), it is a transliteration of the Spanish *reducción*. In the case of the Jesuits in Paraguay, the term reflected their intentions of gathering indigenous South Americans into mission towns (McNaspy 1987:398).

4. Asunción was named for Our Lady of Assumption, the feast corresponding to the day of its founding.

5. According to a recent report conducted by the Inter-American Commission on Human Rights (2009), the Guaraní living in a region known as the Bolivian Chaco are today still the victims of debt bondage and forced labor, contemporary forms of slavery rooted in a historical legacy left by the first Europeans in the region.

6. Once completed, the reductions covered an area that includes parts of present-day Paraguay, Argentina, and Brazil.

7. In addition to the thirty "Guaraní" reductions established along the Paraná and Uruguay rivers, two reductions were established later in the north among groups often referred to as "Tobati-Guaraní" (Ganson 2003:3).

8. On January 5, 2011, the Paraguayan government adopted Guaraní as the official language (alongside Castilian) of Paraguay. Roughly 80 percent of the Paraguayan population speaks Guaraní ("Paraguay: Government Adopts Guaraní Language as an Official Language," http://indigenouspeoplesissues.com, January 7, 2011).

9. Accompanying DeSmet were Fr. Nicholas Point and Fr. Gregory Mengarini, as well as Brothers William Claessens, Charles Huet, and Joseph Specht (DeSmet 1985:12).

10. At the point of contact with the Blackrobes, the Coeur d'Alene referred to themselves as Schitus'umsh, meaning "Those who were found here" or "The discovered people." The name "Coeur d'Alene" was applied to the Schitus'umsh by French-speaking fur trappers and traders. Translated as "heart of an awl," the term referred to what the trappers viewed as the tribe's shrewd trading practices—or, perhaps closer to the truth, their frustration at being unable to swindle the Coeur d'Alene (http://www.cdatribe-nsn.gov/).

11. Johnny Arlee is referring to the group of Iroquois led by Old Ignace, who left the Catholic mission at Caughnawaga in 1812 and settled among the Salish in Montana in 1820 (see chapter 1; Miller 1985:52–53).

12. In 1939, Pope Pius XII successfully eased the restrictions, allowing for Chinese Catholics to attend Confucian ceremonies once again. As a result, the Chinese government began a diplomatic dialogue with the Vatican in 1943 (Minamiki 1985:195).

13. Louise and Martha were sisters of Twisted Earth (aka Joseph Stella'am). Martha's son, Vincent, also became integral to the efforts of the early Rocky Mountain Jesuits, catechizing the youth and becoming a lay leader of sorts. He was so respected among his people that he became head chief during the Steptoe War of 1858, in which Colonel Edward Steptoe and his command were defeated by a force comprising Spokan, Palúus, Yakama, and Coeur d'Alene warriors (Tom Connolly, Olsen interview, 1993).

14. After spring floods ruined food crops, the mission was moved to Cataldo, Idaho, in 1846. In the 1860s a road was built near this site that became a thoroughfare for settlers and gold prospectors, disrupting the solitude and day-to-day operations of the mission. In 1877 they moved to the village of De Smet, near the southern end of Lake Coeur d'Alene, where the Church of the Sacred Heart stands today ("Fr. Tom Connolly: History of the Coeur d'Alenes," www.rockymtnmission.org).

Chapter 3. The Old Indian Hymns

1. We cannot know what Salish songs were sung on this particular occasion, but it is reasonable to conclude, based on Salish song style, that they did not include harmony as defined in musical terms (i.e., two or more different notes sung simultaneously). DeSmet most likely heard monophonic songs sung by many in unison, the cohesive nature of which led him to use the term *harmony* in a nonmusical sense (as in "harmonious"). As Alan Merriam points out in *Ethnomusicology of the Flathead Indians*, in traditional Salish songs, "there is not a single element of Western music to be heard" (1967:137). DeSmet was likely unable to decipher any Salish words contained in the songs, so it remains unclear where his assertion of songs sung "in the praise of God" comes from. What *is* clear is that songs stemming from the spiritual traditions of the Salish quickly fell out of favor with the Jesuits, who actively discouraged everything associated with those traditions, including songs.

2. The city of Spokane Falls officially changed its name to "Spokane" in 1891 (Ruby and Brown 2006:202).

3. Indian Canyon was just west of Hangman Creek, named for the location where fifteen Native Plateau people were hung at the close of the Wright campaign of 1858. The campaign was a response to the Coeur d'Alene War of that year, during which Colonel Edward Steptoe suffered a defeat at the hands of members of numerous Plateau tribes near present-day Rosalia, Washington. Intent on avenging the loss, Wright conducted a thorough onslaught, killing hundreds of horses and destroying all standing crops he could find (Wynecoop 1969:27).

4. Unpublished biographical notes on the life of Mitch Michael, written by Tom Connolly (unpaginated typescript), copy in possession of the author (hereafter cited as Connolly b).

5. Oral accounts suggest that Wildshoe was Colville and was adopted by the Moses family, who moved along with the Michaels from St. Michaels Mission in Peone Prairie to Worley. Wildshoe is an English adaptation of Way-eel-shu-lewh, which means "long ways from the land."

6. The interval might be even greater if one takes into account low-frequency pitches voiced at the beginning and end of melodic glides. These frequencies have a guttural quality, often sung, in the case of a male voice, well below 50 hertz (lower than pitches commonly spoken or sung). I allude to such frequencies in cases where the singer has placed particular emphasis on them; these are shown with an extended marking in red of over a tenth. While written melodic glides of over a tenth do not show the entire interval (an issue of legibility and space), the others do. All pitches were measured in hertz using Praat, a linguistic program designed to analyze and synthesize speech.

7. The transcription also serves as a method of decolonization, freeing elements of Native song style from the confines of European notational constructs. It is important to emphasize that all hymns are sung a cappella and in many instances resist conforming to a set meter. I have chosen meters that most readily accommodate a given performance, but there are times when the melody in a recording moves beyond imposed metrical boundaries, a limitation not of the singers but of the format being used here.

8. Unpublished autobiographical notes written by Tom Connolly (unpaginated typescript), copy in possession of the author (hereafter cited as Connolly a).

9. In 1878, Father Joseph Cataldo moved St. Michael's Mission to the location where Mount St. Michaels sits today. Overlooking northeastern Spokane, Mount St. Michaels opened its doors in 1915 to scholastics pursuing the Jesuit Order. Today it continues to be a place for religious education and training, maintained by members of the Congregation of Mary Immaculate Queen.

10. Eventually, "Qeqs Čšnim" would be sung at wakes for Catholic Native people throughout the Columbia Plateau.

Chapter 4. Song and Power

1. The medicine dance is also commonly referred to as the "winter dance." For a concise overview of its features, see Ray 1939:103.

2. This ceremony has become known variously as the "vision quest," "spirit quest," and "power quest," a deviation from original terms in Native languages to describe similar ceremonies in different communities. Though popularized, appropriated, and often misunderstood within New Age circles, use of the term *vision quest* in Native communities and by Native scholars makes it an appropriate term to use here.

3. Declining power in this way is not historically uncommon. Oral histories maintain that Shining Shirt, the Upper Pend Oreille prophet who along with Circling Raven foretold the coming of the Jesuits, refused power from the spirits that would have enabled him to heal. Instead, they gave him a message to relay about the Blackrobes, a responsibility that would require less of him in return. Interview conducted on February 2, 2008, by Hamill and Connolly.

Chapter 5. Gibson Eli: A Case Study of Song and Power

1. Eli is generally known as "the last medicine man" by many among the Spokan and surrounding tribes.
2. Unpublished biographical notes on the life of Gibson Eli, written by Tom Connolly (unpaginated typescript), copy in possession of the author (hereafter cited as Connolly c).
3. The transcription is based on a recording of the interview, given to me by a genealogist with the Spokane Tribe.
4. For Eli to use the power associated with the song would have required the consent and cooperation of the spirit who granted it in the first place. In this case, the animal spirit appears to have endorsed the shift of ownership from Staneck to Eli.

Chapter 6. Medicine and Miracles

1. The stick game (also known as the hand game) centers on two pairs of "bones." One bone in each pair is striped, the other plain. In general terms, two members from one group hide the bones within their clenched fists while the other side attempts to divine the whereabouts of the unmarked bone, all while drawing from an extensive repertoire of songs.
2. Unpublished biographical notes on the life of Gibson Eli, written by Tom Connolly (unpaginated typescript), copy in possession of the author (hereafter cited as Connolly c).
3. At some point later, Eli shared with Connolly that "daytime was the time of the people. Night was the time for the animals to come out. At the end of the dance, the wolf song is sung again, as the animals head back; the wolf is lonesome because it won't be with the animals again until another night" (Connolly, pers. comm.).
4. See account of the medicine woman and the "fire" in chapter 4.
5. Unpublished biographical notes on the life of Mitch Michael, written by Tom Connolly (unpaginated typescript), copy in possession of the author (hereafter cited as Connolly b).
6. See accounts in chapter 1 referring to song acquisition and the death experience.
7. Contemporary evidence of such occurrences can be readily found in accounts of near-death experiences, known as NDEs (for a cross-cultural list of sources on NDEs, see chapter 1, note 5). Account 2 in

chapter 1 references the introduction of embalming in the Columbia Plateau, which put an end to the resurrection phenomenon and negatively impacted a process of song acquisition.

8. In the early days of the missions, the body was carried to the church by horse-drawn wagon rather than by car, followed by a procession of mourners singing the Indian hymns (Arlee n.d.:5).

9. Music for the funeral mass was, as it is today, negotiable. It might include organ music, contemporary English hymns, a funeral mass in Latin, Indian hymns, or some combination thereof.

10. After the original mission was deemed unsustainable (it was built on a floodplain), Fr. Joseph Joset (Point's successor) selected a site for a new mission on a hill overlooking the Coeur d'Alene River. Known today as the Cataldo Mission, it was built by the Coeur d'Alene under the direction of Fr. Antony Ravalli in 1850. The mission would be short-lived. Without consulting the tribe, President Andrew Johnson ordered the creation of a reservation for the Coeur d'Alene in June 1867. Refusing to give up lands bequeathed by their ancestors, the Coeur d'Alene negotiated an extension of the reservation boundary in 1873. When Congress failed to ratify the reservation later that year, Johnson established it by executive order, ignoring the previous agreement to extend the reservation boundary (Ruby and Brown 1981:262). Owing to the Coeur d'Alene's forced removal, the Mission of the Sacred Heart was relocated once again in 1876, to where it now sits in De Smet, Idaho. Although its days as a mission came to an end in the 1870s, the Cataldo Mission still stands today, carrying the distinction of being the oldest surviving building in the state of Idaho (Frey 2001:65).

11. The canvas was painted by Mitch Michael's cousin, Clara Covington.

12. As a testament to its strength and viability, the sweathouse can be found, in one form or another, throughout North and South America.

Chapter 7. The End and the Afterlife

1. Cornelius Byrne, in unpublished biographical notes on the life of Mitch Michael, written by Tom Connolly (unpaginated typescript), copy in possession of the author (hereafter cited as Connolly b).

2. Unpublished biographical notes on the life of Gibson Eli, written by Tom Connolly (unpaginated typescript), copy in possession of the author (hereafter cited as Connolly c).

3. Ibid.

References

Aguilar, George. 2005. *When the River Ran Wild! Indian Traditions on the Mid-Columbia and the Warm Springs Reservation.* Portland: Oregon Historical Society Press.

Amnesty International. 2004. *Draft UN Declaration on the Rights of Indigenous Peoples: No Excuses—International Recognition and Protection of the Human Rights of Indigenous Peoples Long Overdue.* London: Amnesty International, International Secretariat.

Aoki, Haruo. 1994. *Nez Perce Dictionary.* Berkeley: University of California Press.

Arlee, Johnny. 2001. *Qʷelm u Nčʼawmn: A Collection of Hymns and Prayers in the Flathead-Kalispel-Spokane Indian Language; International Phonetic Alphabet Version.* Pablo, Mont.: Salish Kootenai College Press.

———. n.d. "Wakes, Funerals, and Feast Days." Unpublished pamphlet. Flathead Cultural Committee.

Bailey, Lee W. 2001. "A 'Little Death': The Near-Death Experience and Tibetan Delogs." *Journal of Near-Death Studies* 19 (3): 139–59.

Beck, Thomas E., and Janet E. Colli. 2003. "A Quantum Biomechanical Basis for Near Death Life Reviews." *Journal of Near-Death Studies* 21 (3): 169–89.

Bell, Stuart, Steve Gibbons, Debra Sequeira, and Jose Zevallos. 2007. "ILO Convention 169 and the Private Sector: Questions and Answers for IFC Clients." International Finance Corporation.

Bengoa, José, Volodymyr Grygorovitch Boutkevitch, Stanislav Valentinovich Chernichenko, Asbjorn Eide, Osman El-Hajjé, Ribot Hatano, and Christy Ezim Mbonu. 1995. *International Decade of the World's Indigenous People: Draft Resolution.* Geneva: United Nations.

Berliner, Paul. 1978. *The Soul of Mbira: Music and Traditions of the Shona People of Zimbabwe.* Berkeley: University of California Press.

Bischoff, William N. 1945. *The Jesuits in Old Oregon, 1840–1940.* Caldwell, Idaho: Caxton Printers.

Bohlman, Philip V., Edith L. Blumhofer, and Maria M. Chow. 2006. *Music in American Religious Experience.* Oxford: Oxford University Press.

Brockey, Liam M. 2007. *Journey to the East: The Jesuit Mission to China, 1579–1724.* Cambridge, Mass.: Belknap Press of Harvard University Press.

Cadena, Marisol de la, and Orin Starn (eds.). 2007. *Indigenous Experience Today.* Oxford: Berg.

Caraman, Philip. 1976. *The Lost Paradise: An Account of the Jesuits in Paraguay, 1607–1768.* New York: Seabury Press.

Carriker, Robert C. 1995. *Father Peter John DeSmet: Jesuit in the West.* Norman: University of Oklahoma Press.

Christian Brothers. 1885. *The Catholic Youth's Hymn Book: Containing the Hymns of the Seasons and Festivals of the Year, and an Extensive*

Collection of Sacred Melodies; to Which Are Added an Easy Mass, Vespers, and Motets for Benediction, Arr. with a Special View to the Wants of Catholic Schools and Choirs. New York: P. O'Shea.

Connolly, Thomas E. 1958. *Quáy-Lem U En-Chów-Men: A Collection of Hymns and Prayers in the Flathead-Kalispel-Spokane Indian Languages.* Spokane, Wash.: Bernard J. Topel.

Connolly, Thomas E. (ed.), and Clarence Woodcock (rev.). 1983. *Quáy-lem u en-chów-men: A Collection of Hymns and Prayers in the Flathead-Kalispel-Spokane Indian Language.* Pablo, Mont.: Salish Kootenai College.

DeSmet, Pierre-Jean. 1905. *Life, Letters and Travels of Father Pierre-Jean DeSmet, S.J., 1801–1873.* Vol. 1. Edited by Hiram M. Chittenden and Alfred Talbot Richardson. New York: Harper.

———. *New Indian Sketches.* 1985. Edited by Edward J. Kowrach. Fairfield, Wash.: Ye Galleon Press. First published in 1863 by D. and J. Sadlier and Co.

Drury, Clifford Merrill. 1936. *Henry Harmon Spalding.* Caldwell, Idaho: Caxton Printers.

Dubois, Cora Alice. 1938. *The Feather Cult of the Middle Columbia.* Menasha, Wis.: George Banta Publishing.

Feld, Steven. 1982. *Sound and Sentiment: Birds, Weeping, Poetics, and Song in Kaluli Expression.* Philadelphia: University of Pennsylvania Press.

Fenske, Elizabeth W. 1990. "The Near Death Experience: An Ancient Truth, a Modern Mystery." *Journal of Near Death Studies* 8 (3): 129–49.

Fortier, Ted. 2002. *Religion and Resistance in the Encounter between the Coeur D'Alene Indians and Jesuit Missionaries.* Lewiston, N.Y.: Edwin Mellen Press.

Frey, Rodney. 2001. *Landscape Traveled by Coyote and Crane: The World of the Schitsu'umsh, Coeur d'Alene Indians.* Seattle: University of Washington Press.

Friedson, Steven M. 1996. *Dancing Prophets: Musical Experience in Tumbuka Healing.* Chicago: University of Chicago Press.

Fülöp-Miller, René, F. S. Flint, and D. F. Tait. 1930. *The Power and Secret of the Jesuits.* New York: Viking Press.

Ganson, Barbara A. 2003. *The Guaraní under Spanish Rule in the Río de la Plata.* Stanford: Stanford University Press.

Gaudry, Adam. 2011. "Insurgent Research." *Wicazo Sa Review* 26 (1): 113–36.

Gott, Richard. 1993. *Land Without Evil: Utopian Journeys across the South American Watershed.* London: Verso.

Hamill, Chad. 2008. "Songs from Spirit: Power and Prayer in the Columbia Plateau." PhD dissertation, University of Colorado. (Ann Arbor, Mich.: University Microfilms, 2009.)

Harden, Blaine. 1996. *A River Lost: The Life and Death of the Columbia.* New York: W. W. Norton.

Hsia, R. P. 2005. *The World of Catholic Renewal, 1540–1770*. New Approaches to European History. New York: Cambridge University Press.

Inter-American Commission on Human Rights. 2009. "Captive Communities: Situation of the Guaraní Indigenous People and Contemporary Forms of Slavery in the Bolivian Chaco." Organization of American States. Online link, http://indigenouspeoplesissues.com.

Irwin, Lee. 1994. *The Dream Seekers: Native American Visionary Traditions of the Great Plains*. Norman: University of Oklahoma Press.

Jankowsky, Richard C. 2010. *Stambeli: Music, Trance, and Alterity in Tunisia*. Chicago: University of Chicago Press.

Josephy, Alvin M. 1965. *The Nez Perce Indians and the Opening of the Northwest*. New Haven, Conn.: Yale University Press.

Kan, Sergei. 1985. "Russian Orthodox Brotherhoods among the Tlingit: Missionary Goals and Native Response." *Ethnohistory* 32 (3): 196–223.

Kapchan, Deborah A., and Pauline Turner Strong. 1999. "Theorizing the Hybrid." *Journal of American Folklore* 112 (445): 239–253.

Leopold, Anita M., and Jeppe S. Jensen. 2005. *Syncretism in Religion: A Reader*. New York: Routledge.

Marett, Allan. 2005. *Songs, Dreamings, and Ghosts: The Wangga of North Australia*. Middletown, Conn.: Wesleyan University Press.

McAllester, David. 2006. "Reminiscences of the Early Days." *Ethnomusicology* 50 (2): 199–203.

McIntosh, Ian, with John Bowen, Marcus Colchester, and Dan Rosengren. 2002. "Defining Oneself, and Being Defined as, Indigenous." *Anthropology Today* 18 (3): 23–24.

McNaspy, C. J. 1987. "The Archaeology of the Paraguay Reductions (1609–1767)." *World Archaeology* 18 (3): 398–410.

McWhorter, Lucullus Virgil, and Ruth Birgitta Anderson Bordin. 1952. *Hear Me, My Chiefs! Nez Perce History and Legend*. Caldwell, Idaho: Caxton Printers.

Mengarini, Gregory. 1977. *Recollections of the Flathead Mission: Containing Brief Observations, Both Ancient and Contemporary, Concerning This Particular Nation*. Edited and translated by Gloria Ricci Lothrop. Glendale, Calif.: A. H. Clark.

Merriam, Alan P. 1965. "The Importance of Song in the Flathead Vision Quest." *Ethnomusicology* 9 (2): 91–99.

———. 1967. *Ethnomusicology of the Flathead Indians*. Chicago: Aldine Publishing.

Miller, Christopher L. 1985. *Prophetic Worlds: Indians and Whites on the Columbia Plateau*. New Brunswick, N.J.: Rutgers University Press.

Minamiki, George. 1985. *The Chinese Rites Controversy: From Its Beginning to Modern Times*. Chicago: Loyola University Press.

Moody, Raymond A. 1977. *Reflections on Life After Life*. Harrisburg, Penn.: Stackpole Books.

Moses, L. G. 1985. "The Father Tells Me So! Wovoka: The Ghost Dance Prophet." *American Indian Quarterly* 9 (3): 335–51.

Muratori, Lodovico A. (ed.). 1759. *A Relation of the Missions of Paraguay: Wrote Originally in Italian, by Mr. Muratori, and Now Done into English from the French Translation, with the Relations of Father Cagetan [Cajetan] Cattaneo.* Translated into French by F. E. Lourmel. London: J. Marmaduke.

Nawrot, Piotr. 2004. "Teaching of Music and the Celebration of Liturgical Events in the Jesuit Reductions." *Anthropos* 99 (1): 73–83.

Nettl, Bruno. 1989. *Blackfoot Musical Thought: Comparative Perspectives.* Kent, Ohio: Kent State University Press.

———. 2005. *The Study of Ethnomusicology: Thirty-One Issues and Concepts.* Urbana: University of Illinois Press.

Niezen, Ronald. 2003. *The Origins of Indigenism: Human Rights and the Politics of Identity.* Berkeley: University of California Press.

O'Connor, James. n.d. "1888–1891: The Flathead Indians." *Records of the American Catholic Historical Society of Philadelphia* 3: 85–110.

Olsen, Loran. 1974. "External Influences in Nez Perce Song." Paper presented at the annual meeting of the American Folklore Society, Portland, Oregon, October 31.

———. 2001. *Qillóowawya: Hitting the Rawhide: Serenade Songs from the Nez Perce Music Archive.* Seattle: Northwest Interpretive Association.

Olsen, Loran, and Thomas Connolly, S.J. 2001. "Musical Syncretism at the Missions." *Native American Studies* 15 (1): 13–17.

Olsen, Loran, and Sol Webb. 1972. *Nez Perce Songs of Historical Significance: As Sung by "Sol" Webb.* Lapwai: Nez Perce Indian Tribe of Idaho, in cooperation with the Music Department, Washington State University.

O'Malley, John W. 2000. *Trent and All That: Renaming Catholicism in the Early Modern Era.* Cambridge, Mass.: Harvard University Press.

Palladino, L. B. 1922. *Indian and White in the Northwest: A History of Catholicity in Montana.* Lancaster, Penn.: Wickersham Publishing Company. Originally published by J. Murphy, Baltimore, Md., 1894.

Partoll, Albert J. 1951. *The Flathead-Salish Indian Name in Montana Nomenclature.* Helena, Mont.: n.p.

Peterson, Jacqueline, and Laura L. Peers. 1993. *Sacred Encounters: Father DeSmet and the Indians of the Rocky Mountain West.* Norman: University of Oklahoma Press.

Point, Nicolas. 1967. *Wilderness Kingdom, Indian Life in the Rocky Mountains: 1840–1847; The Journals and Paintings of Nicolas Point.* Translated by Joseph P. Donnelly. New York: Holt, Rinehart and Winston.

Project to Promote ILO Policy on Indigenous and Tribal Peoples, and International Labour Office. 2000. *ILO Convention on Indigenous and Tribal Peoples, 1989 (No. 169): Manual.* Geneva: ILO.

Ray, Verne F. 1933. *The Sanpoil and the Nespelem Salishan Peoples of Northeastern Washington.* Seattle: University of Washington Press.

———. 1936. "The Kolaskin Cult: A Prophet Movement in 1870 in Northeastern Washington." *American Anthropologist* 38: 67–75.

————. 1939. *Cultural Relations in the Plateau of Northwestern America*. Los Angeles: Southwest Museum.

Relander, Click. 1956. *Drummers and Dreamers: The Story of Smowhala the Prophet and His Nephew Puck Hyah Toot, the Last Prophet of the Nearly Extinct River People, the Last Wanapums*. Caldwell, Idaho: Caxton Printers.

Ring, Kenneth. 1984. *Heading Toward Omega: In Search of the Meaning of the Near-Death Experience*. New York: Quill/William Morrow.

Ring, Kenneth, and Evelyn Valarino. 1998. *Lessons from the Light: What We Can Learn From the Near-Death Experience*. New York: Insight Books.

Ruby, Robert H., and John A. Brown. 1981. *Indians of the Pacific Northwest: A History*. Norman: University of Oklahoma Press.

————. 2006. *The Spokane Indians, Children of the Sun*. Expanded edition. Civilization of the American Indians 104. Norman: University of Oklahoma Press.

Samuels, David W. 2004. *Putting a Song on Top of It: Expression and Identity on the San Carlos Apache Reservation*. Tucson: University of Arizona Press.

Seeger, Anthony. 1987. *Why Suyá Sing: A Musical Anthropology of an Amazonian People*. Cambridge: Cambridge University Press.

Seeger, Charles. 1958. "Prescriptive and Descriptive Music-Writing." *Musical Quarterly* 44 (2): 184–95.

Seltice, Joseph. 1990. *Saga of the Coeur d'Alene Indians: An Account of Chief Joseph Seltice*. Edited by Edward J. Kowrach and Thomas E. Connolly. Fairfield, Wash.: Ye Galleon Press.

Smith, Linda Tuhiwai. 1999. *Decolonizing Methodologies: Research and Indigenous Peoples*. London: Zed Books.

Sommer, Rebecca. 2007. *Discussions on the UN Declaration on the Rights of Indigenous Peoples: A Draft Work-in-Progress Lobby Video*. Sommer Films.

Stamatopoulou, Elsa. 2009. *State of the World's Indigenous Peoples*. New York: United Nations Permanent Forum on Indigenous Issues.

Stern, Theodore. 1960. "A Umatilla Prophet Cult." In *Men and Cultures*, edited by Anthony C. Wallace, 346–50. Philadelphia: University of Pennsylvania Press.

Steward, Julian H. 1963. *Handbook of South American Indians*. New York: Cooper Square Publishers.

Trafzer, Clifford E. (ed.). 1986. *American Indian Prophets*. Newcastle, Calif.: Sierra Oak Publishing.

United Nations. 1982. *Report of the Working Group on Indigenous Populations on Its 1st Session*. Geneva: United Nations.

————. 1983. *Programme for the Decade for Action to Combat Racism and Racial Discrimination*. New York: United Nations, Department of Public Information.

————. 1994. *Indigenous People: International Decade, 1995–2004*. New York: United Nations, Department of Public Information.

Walker, Deward E. 1967. *Mutual Cross-Utilization of Economic Resources in the Plateau: An Example from Aboriginal Nez Perce Fishing Practices*. Pullman: Washington State University, Laboratory of Anthropology.

————. 1985. *Conflict and Schism in Nez Percé Acculturation: A Study of Religion and Politics*. Moscow: University of Idaho Press.

------. 1989. *Witchcraft and Sorcery of the American Native Peoples*. Moscow: University of Idaho Press.

Wilkes, Charles. 1845. *Narrative of the United States Exploring Expedition, during the Years 1838, 1839, 1840, 1841, 1842*. 4 vols. Philadelphia: Lea and Blanchard.

Wynecoop, David C. 1969. *Children of the Sun: A History of the Spokane Indians*. Wellpinit, Wash.: published by the author.

Index

"ʔa Spuʔús" ("Hymn to the Sacred Heart"), 48–53

accomodation, cultural, 3–4, 35–36. *See also* repression, cultural
Adolph (Squilsquilskape, Red Feather), *33*
agriculture, 19–20
Aldmaklen (Victor), *33*
Alexander (Canachkkstchin), *33*
Alexander, Jackson, 135–36
Alexander, Lavinia, *46, 47,* 74–83, 92–93, 94–95, 135
American Anthropological Association, 140
angels, 110
animal spirits: Catholicism and, 110–11, 130; Eli and, 66–68, 85–90,
    98–101, 142; hymns and, 62; images of, *34–35;* Susan Michael and,
    74–75, 78–83; power and, 64–68, 87–88; songs and, 71–74, 75–76,
    82–83; Stanek and, 100–101; stick games and, 98–99, 103–6; Tomeo
    and, 66–68. *See also* spirit guides
Antelope, Morris, 32–33
anthropological studies, 12, 140–41
Apache people, 2
Arlee, Johnny, 111: on hymns, 57, 119; recordings of, 51, *52, 53, 54, 129;*
    on repression by missionaries, 32; on wakes, 111, 113–14, 116, 123
Asian missions, 35–36
Asunción, Paraguay, 27
Australians, indigenous, 72–73

baptisms, 26, 36, 103
bear medicine, 74, 80–81, 83
Berliner, Paul, 73
Bible, 20–22, 109
Bighead, 20
Big Smoke, Baptiste, 56, 60, 111
Blackrobes. *See* Jesuit missionaries
Bolaños, Luis de, 27, 29
Bonaventure (Chinmitkasy), *33*
Bone, Medor, 45
Buck and Doe (Spokane, WA), 106
Byrne, Cornelius, 78, *115,* 125

Canachkkstchin (Alexander), *33*
cancer, 92–97
Cárdenes, Bernardino, 30
Cataldino, José, 29
Cataldo, Joseph, 44, *126*
Catholicism: animal spirits and, 110–11, 130; conversions to, 3, 29,